SATAN, SUICIDE, AND SANCTUARY

Dawn Early

ISBN 979-8-88851-508-2 (Paperback)
ISBN 979-8-88851-510-5 (Hardcover)
ISBN 979-8-88851-509-9 (Digital)

All biblical citations were taken from the 1991 NIV to the most current NIV translation, unless otherwise noted.

Covenant Books
11661 Hwy 707
Murrells Inlet, SC 29576
www.covenantbooks.com

In memory of the late Dr. James Smith, known simply as Brother Jim. Without his sound biblical teaching, I do not know if I would have found my way back to God. Not only was he an outstanding preacher/teacher, but he also exemplified in his daily life the love of Jesus. I am forever grateful for all he instilled in me throughout the years he was here among us.

To my Robby, who is truly my soulmate and partner in life. There are no words to describe the love I have for you. You have been by my side through the good, bad, and ugly. You are strong and proud, but equally humble, and that is a rare combination. You have my heart.

She lay down to die:
Surely that was better than staying alive.
She could feel herself sinking into an abyss,
that was ominous and dark.
Slowly she could feel the cold embracing her:
Finally, the pain was leaving as she slipped into unconsciousness.
She was me.

—Dawn Renee

As I am sitting here writing this, I only have a vague remembrance of the day I attempted suicide. January 13, 2020, was a day that will forever be a blur. Looking back three years later, I try to piece the day together in my mind, but there are gaps. I may not remember that day clearly, but I remember how I got there.

I remember the intense pain of betrayal, the constant bullying, and seemingly not having anyone to turn to. I completely spun out, and as my counselor told me later, my brain could no longer cope with the happenings going on in my life. The coping side of my brain shut down. I had never felt like that before, and hopefully, I never will again. You may ask, how does that even happen? It was not a quick onset, but more like a gradual process of things continually piling up. The pile of misfortunes got to be so heavy, I felt like I was drowning in darkness. As a follower of Christ, I could not understand why all these things were happening almost simultaneously. My faith was being tested in ways I never knew existed. And believe me when I say I had a very dysfunctional childhood. But I had overcome the difficult experiences of growing up. It was a painful journey not only from the abuses that occurred in my childhood, but also from mistakes I made trying to survive. I eventually married a beautiful man, and together we started building a life together.

Our journey has had many bumps in the road; but together we became followers of Christ, raised our children in the church, and forged godly friendships. Then we got to the aforementioned day— the day I decided to end it all. I wanted to forget the three years prior: the hurt, the person I was becoming, the caring for a bipolar parent, and, the worst feeling of them all, the betrayal by Christian friends.

I have wanted to write my experiences not to persecute anyone, but so that others may recognize signs when you need to walk away from harmful situations. When to walk away from the oppression bestowed on you by a job, people, or anything that beats down on you mentally. I want to express my thoughts on my anger with God for allowing the season I had to face. I want to feel free to say that it is not shameful when your coping skills have had enough. I want it to be known that there is a difference between religion and Christianity.

I hope you enjoy, learn, and grow as I share my experience of a suicide attempt. I want to share not only my experience of this time, but my husband's thoughts as well. It's a journey I hope that will inspire you to overcome and not travel the path I went down. I have written this as a daily devotional, to incorporate scriptures with experiences I have gone through. I will share the good and bad with all the many life changes along the way. Please do not laugh at all the school and job changes.

> There is a time for everything, and a season
> for every activity under the heavens:
>
> a time to be born and a time to die,
> a time to plant and a time to uproot,
> a time to kill and a time to heal,
> a time to tear down and a time to build,
> a time to weep and a time to laugh,
> a time to mourn and a time to dance,
> a time to scatter stones and a time to gather them,
> a time to embrace and a time to refrain from
>   embracing,
> a time to search and a time to give up,
> a time to keep and a time to throw away,
> a time to tear and a time to mend,
> a time to be silent and a time to speak,
> a time to love and a time to hate,
> a time for war and a time for peace. (Ecclesiastes
>   3:1–8 NIV)

I started with this scripture and will reference it throughout this book due to its eternal essence, meaning God knows the seasons we will go through; and although we may not like where we are, He has a plan for us. I like the Amplified Bible's version of verse 1:

> There is a season (a time appointed) for everything and a time for every delight, an event or purpose under heaven.

I will be honest. I don't like some of the seasons I have endured, and sometimes I feel like I am in a perpetual season of being torn down. Out of the four seasons of nature, I feel like I have had more winter than I can endure. It can be cold, dreary, and depressing and hard to find the beauty. But the darkness can be overcome, and you can find beauty again.

I have no clue what season you are in, but I can assure you that we all go through all kinds of seasons. If you are not a believer in Christ, you may find the rationale of how I depend on God strange, but I encourage you to come along on this journey of finding the good in the ugliness.

DAY 1

Learned Behavior

For you created in my inmost being;
you knit me together in my mother's womb.
I praise you because I am fearfully and wonderfully made;
your works are wonderful,
I know that full well.
—Psalm 139:13–14 NIV

I am going to share a little of my childhood so you can understand my views, mentality, and coping skills. Sometimes I think, *Why am*

I here? I read this scripture and think, *God, You created me, but why? Why! Why! Why!*

As a child, I learned early on how to walk on eggshells. I learned to keep most of my opinions and thoughts to myself, from absolute fear of being chastised. I was conceived out of wedlock, so I have struggled with being an accident. And I have struggled with why God created me, since the scripture says I was wonderfully made.

I remember vague snippets in my very early years of the manic happy moments and the low depressive moments of my mother. I can remember the tantrums of her screaming, her ripping up the Christmas presents, the periods when she was gone for days at a time, and then the crash would come, and she would just stay in bed. I remember well the physical and mental abuse. I remember the exact spot where my daddy told me they were getting a divorce. Add to that it was the 1970s, and of course there was partying and us children being left to our own devices if a babysitter could not be found. And I had a younger sister, whom I had to learn to take care of. And I did till the day I walked out of that chaos at the age of eighteen. Needless to say, I walked straight into another mess, but we can discuss that later.

As I write this, all the negative and depressing memories come flooding back. They make me want to stop writing and shut down my computer and abandon this altogether. But I can feel the Holy Spirit nudging me softly every day to keep writing. On good days and bad days, there is this soft, gentle whisper in my soul, urging me to stay on this path. It absolutely terrifies me to open some of the doors I have closed off. It makes me feel vulnerable and weak that I am not always in complete control. I would suspect most want to feel like they are in control of their own life and destiny. But the truth is not a single person in the world knows what is just around the corner.

When I look at the scripture for today, I still find myself asking God, why am I here? Sometimes I just scream that question at the top of my lungs. But I remind myself He is the creator, not me. That can humble you very quickly.

I can assure you, I constantly ask why me a lot of days, but I would like to get to a place where I can say, "Prepare me, Lord, for the day. Prepare me for whatever comes my way, good or bad." Truthfully speaking, I probably will fail on the bad days.

As you go through today, simply ask the Lord to lead you.

Ask Him whom you might be able to minister to by sharing a past hurt.

Hand over your heartaches that you are bitter about and ask Him to give you a fresh word from the Scripture to start the healing process.

These three requests look small on paper, but I know how big they are in the world. I also know the healing process from past traumas take time. There never is a quick fix; but we have a master healer, who loves us, created us, and will help us through our journey in a sinful world.

Do you believe you are wonderfully made by God? Why or why not?

DAY 2

Living in the Slimy Pit

He lifted me out of the slimy pit, out of the mud and mire, he
set my feet on a rock and gave me a firm place to stand.
—Psalm 40:2 NIV

As mentioned earlier, I left home at eighteen and just moved right on into my next debacle. And what a failure the next phase of my life was. I was a babe trying to live in an adult world with dysfunctional views and behavior. I married a man who was twelve years older than me just to escape the horrors of my homelife. For a while it was good, but then one night, I was awakened, and he told me we had to leave. All I took was what I could pack in a suitcase. I had no idea why we left so abruptly at the time. I was scared and had no support network to call or get help. We literally drove from place to place sleeping either in a car or sometimes in a cheap motel. Somehow, we managed to find someone to take us in in Memphis.

We both got jobs, and I thought things were getting better. Then the car was repossessed, and the truth came out. We had been moving around because he owed large amounts of money to people. I had never felt so alone in my entire life. I knew who God was, but I did not know God. I knew nothing about praying and reading the Scripture. So I spiraled straight down into a dark and scary pit of sinful behavior.

We moved several more times, and neither of us were angels. You may ask why I stayed. I was simply trying to survive. All I knew was what I had learned as a child, which was suffering through pain. Then we had a child, and I knew that somehow, I had to get out of that pit.

My mother was no help, and my father had a life with another family, so I felt like I had no one. I will never forget the day when I finally made that phone call to my daddy and his wife. I was depressed, was beaten down, and could barely take care of myself, much less my daughter. But I knew I had to escape the life I was living or I would be dead, or worse, my daughter would be. I walked out of that life literally skin and bones, and God put me in the place I needed to be, even though I had no clue at the time.

It was not a bed of roses by escaping the life I was in. There was an ugly divorce and custody battle. A period where my daughter was across state lines, and I could not get her back. I got a job, rented a house, and waited for a court date. The wait was not easy, but it came, and I got custody of my daughter.

I did not know it at the time, but God was working hard getting me out of my slimy pit and giving me a firm place to stand. He put me in the place I needed to be at twenty-two years old. I was so young, but I had some serious baggage still weighing me down.

My prayer for you is that if you are in a pit, you ask God to help you find a way out.

Do you believe God can remove you from your pit?

Do you think you are not worthy for God to help you?

Do you think if you get out of your pit that you will not be able to move forward?

I still struggle with these questions at times. But do not be afraid to admit you need help. God can provide it in ways we never imagined. But it is a constant battle within us to keep the faith and be obedient to him.

DAY 3

Putting Down New Roots

For I know the plans I have for you, declares the Lord, plans to prosper you and not to harm you, plans to give you hope and a future.
—Jeremiah 29:11 NIV

Let me preface by saying I had lived like a gypsy my entire life. Before I was seven, we had lived in about a dozen places. I would pack and unpack my belongings quite often throughout my childhood. It's funny how you have friends, but they never really know what goes on in your life. I had become so guarded in sharing my true feelings with anyone that I felt like I lived two different lives. So when I came to live in a rural county in Mississippi, trust me when I say I had no intentions of staying longer than to get back on my feet.

I almost laugh when I read the aforementioned verse from Jeremiah. I did not even know that verse existed. But God knew I had had enough of the uprooting season, and He was leading me into a season of being planted. He had a future for me. He had plans for me.

In case you forgot, my name is Dawn, and I met a man with the last name Early. At the time, it was cute and sweet, but now I know it was a God thing. He put this man in my path to be the calm in my storm. And I can assure you my storms were brutal at times. Only God could put a dysfunctional, free-roaming young woman with a young man, who had lived pretty much his entire life in the exact

6

spot. We were polar opposites in just about everything, but somehow, we worked well together.

We married and started building a life together with a three-year-old in tow. And we had a lot of fun in those early years horse-shoeing every Saturday night into the wee hours of Sunday. There is no surprise here that church was sporadic at best. We would drag sometimes at four in the morning and would sleep late on Sunday. Occasionally we would make it to church with Robby's grandmother. But that was the extent of our spiritual relationship with God.

Fast forward six years and we were a nice little family of four. But still no church life. It was not out of rebellion, but out of not knowing what a true relationship with God was. But God had plans for our family, and He brought us to Him through a van ministry a local church had started. Our children were nine and two at the time when we were approached about our daughter being able to go on the van to church. We let her go every Sunday, and God started nudging us that we should all be in church as a family. That nudge took us to a spiritual journey that was humbling, joyous, hard, and eye opening, to say the least. It's a journey that allowed us to start on our spiritual roots.

We were saved and baptized, as were our children. We studied the Bible intensely, especially me. I was soaking all of it up like a sponge. I was finally finding answers for my existence on this planet. I absolutely could not get enough. At the time, we had a preacher who had such great insight and discernment, and he helped many of us on our spiritual journey.

Through Brother Jim's guidance, Robby would go through music seminary and go on to become a minister of music and later an ordained minister. Two others would go through seminary and become pastors; I went through two years of seminary in biblical teaching and taught various ages. It was such a spiritual high even with the obstacles along the way. We formed beautiful friendships. There was wonderful fellowship, mission trips, church socials, etc. Writing this down has made all kinds of emotions surface. Some I wanted to feel again and some that make me sad because of how some things ended. I am so thankful that for those ten years, God was growing those roots deep. I would need that foundation later in life. But no earthly foundation is without cracks, and I can assure you Satan will find them. He found my weakest crack: low self-esteem from all the past trauma in my childhood. And I never saw it coming, but God did. Remember He has a plan for us.

Reread Ecclesiastes 3:1–8 and see if you can find the season you are in. Ask yourself if you are on the right spiritual path in that season. Do you think your season is good or bad?

Do you believe the scripture for today? I can tell you I struggle with this scripture. It is the hardest scripture for me to comprehend. I find myself again asking why I must go through things that are oppressive, hard, and unfair. I have to remind myself daily that we live in a fallen world, and nothing is perfect.

How can we believe this scripture then? Look at the next verses 12 and 13 in Jeremiah 29.

> Then you will call upon me and come and pray to me, and I will listen to you. You will seek me and find me when you seek me with all your heart. (NIV)

We put so much emphasis on verse 11 about what God has promised us that we miss those second two verses. We have a responsibility to Him as well. We are to seek him every day and pray to Him every single day from the heart. Life is hard and unfair, to say the least, but we were never promised it would be easy.

DAY 4

How the Wilderness Journey Began

*Dear friends, do not believe every spirit, but test the
spirits to see whether they are from God, because many
false prophets have gone out into the world.*
—1 John 4:1 NIV

I have laid the foundation of how I was raised, how I came to Christ and the spiritual mountaintop of solid biblical teachings. Today I will start laying the foundation of how my journey began in what I call the wilderness period.

For years, my husband and I poured ourselves in the church and the Word of Christ, but sometimes outside influences can hinder your walk with Christ. I remember Brother Jim always telling us to study the Scripture. If you hear something said in a sermon, go back and read the Word to make sure it is true. He always said never rely on man, but the Word of God. When he left our church, I remember crying my eyes out. He truly lived the way he preached, and unfortunately, not all do. Robby and I both learned after that there are many different maturity levels among preachers. And some personalities don't mix well with others. He resigned as the music minister, and we changed churches twice. We had good and not-so-good experiences among those few years. I live in a small community, so I will not go into much detail, as I do not want to unintentionally hurt the ones who supported and loved us.

During this time, I had left my bookkeeping job and had opened my own photography studio, and it started consuming my time. And I went back to school to become a paramedic. I started backing off from the Scriptures, because quite frankly, I was not getting spiritually fed like I was used to. Around the same time, Robby's job was more demanding, and we started drifting apart. All these things started forming cracks in the foundation of our faith, in our church, and worst in our marriage. And then one day we found ourselves without a church at all and not by our choice. It was a miserable time for us. And for the first time in almost twenty years, we did not have a church home. We were so numb and hurt we just both shut down.

These things did not happen in an instant, but over a course of nine years. Instead of clinging to God's Word, we started letting bitterness take root. For me, it was constantly doubting myself and my judgment in people. The reality was that I was not wrong about people; it was that others did not acknowledge the unspiritual side of people. Do not get me wrong here. I am far from perfect. But with the way I grew up, I learned from an early age to pick up on certain traits people may possess. As the scripture for today says, you should test the spirits of others. But you cannot make people see how others are; they must see for themselves. And I could not understand why God would allow people to be blinded by things that were unholy, that is until the day I was blindsided by people whom I loved deeply in Christ. We will discuss that later.

From the hurt and humiliation that we felt, we did not step into another church for at least a year. I was drained mentally and spiritually. And things were only going to get worse unbeknownst to me.

If I could step back in time, I would bury myself in God's Word, and my knees would be calloused from crying out to God. But I learned from those mistakes the hard way, by turning my back on my beliefs.

I would like for you to examine everything in your life with God. Ask Him to give you discernment on how to react to new things. Ask Him to guide you in new relationships. Ask Him to take blindfolds off when it comes to the ones we love.

These are questions we need to ask ourselves.

Have I prayed enough to know if a situation is spirit led or led by me?

Have I overlooked ungodly traits in people I know just so I could fit in?

Do I give my best to God or the world?

What are ways I can better my relationship with God?

Do I read the Scripture for myself, instead of taking it for granted that it was told or taught to me correctly?

DAY 5

The Tale of Three Bibles

The fear of the Lord is the beginning of knowledge,
but fools despise wisdom and discipline.

—Proverbs 1:7 NIV

I have had three Bibles over the past twenty-four years. The first one I reference as the good years. I read, wrote notes, and underlined scriptures in that Bible for twelve years. This Bible was used in church, at home, for multiple Bible studies, on mission trips, and in seminary. The pages are literally falling out of it. But I still pull it out to read quotes or thoughts I jotted down about specific scriptures. It tells the story of a woman who was soaking in God's Word like a sponge. Nearly every page has something underlined or written on it.

The second Bible I used for nine years. I call it the wilderness Bible. When I go back and read the things I wrote, I see how bad I was struggling in every aspect of my life. Here is an example of how I felt at the time:

> Search my heart: It is not that great right now. The struggle is real right now. I have no true church family, I have no blood family that truly cares, and I have no true friends. My marriage is not great right now. I need to know if it is me that is the repulsive one. I need you so much now.

I wrote those words at the beginning of Psalm 139. This particular Bible is a reminder to me that you can go from having knowledge to acting a fool when you do not fear the Lord. Somewhere in those years, I started living more secular than spiritual. I had lost that thirst of knowledge for God. I had stepped out of one world into another. I went back to school to become a paramedic, and that put me on a roller-coaster ride I was not prepared for. Why? Because I was not in the Word. I was not praying consistently. I was wondering around in the wilderness like the Israelites.

The third Bible, I bought in 2020. It is in a sense my recovery Bible. When Robby was asked to go back to a church we had previously attended, at first the answer was no. But God was working hard on us, and he ultimately decided to go back as music minister. When he went and talked with the committee, he was brutally honest that we were not the same people from the things we had been through, especially me. My faith was weak. I was broken, and I absolutely did not want to trust anyone again. But we obeyed God and went to the bookstore with a mission to buy new Bibles for a fresh start. I pray I look back one day at this Bible, and it will read like my first one. Recovery from being broken is not easy. But when it involves people you loved and trusted, the level of hurt, anger, and sadness is unbearable.

You can literally see three seasons of my Christian life referenced with these three Bibles. So I ask you, which one of these Bibles would you consider yourself in right now?

Are you learning? Are you being rebellious? Are you recovering from your wilderness journey?

Which area would you consider to be the hardest, rebellion or recovery?

For me, I am constantly asking God how I can keep moving forward. I will be honest; it is hard to quit secular habits. The Holy Spirit must be worn out from our constant battles. I ask for forgiveness constantly. So for me, recovering from all my battle scars, either self-inflicted or from others, is the hardest thing I am doing. As we journey through the past five years, hopefully you will not get to the point I did.

DAY 6

Let the Bullying Begin

The entire law is summed up in a single command: "Love your neighbor as yourself." If you keep on biting and devouring each other, watch out or you will be destroyed by each other.
—Galatians 5:14–15 NIV

I have to say when I started out to become a paramedic and got a job as an EMT-B, I was not expecting the spiraling cascade of events that were going to take place. And what is worse, I was warned by my husband that the work environment had drastically changed since I had last worked in the public. Do not get me wrong. I had been working with people in the photography industry a long time, but I was the boss. And what could go wrong, working under a company with Christian leadership? Sadly, things can go immensely wrong.

After I became a Christian, I started healing over my dysfunctional childhood. I prayed over a lot of horrific things. I also prayed that God would take away the bad habits that I had developed, and He did. I wanted to be free from my past transgressions and move on with my life in the Spirit of Christ. The scripture referenced here was hard for me, as were others, to accept. But I learned that love is a powerful gift from God. And we are to try to love like He loves us. I took that to heart.

Paramedic school was an eye-opener into how the generations below mine were. I became aware that the respect for your elders was virtually gone. There seems to be no loyalty except to one's own self. They openly talk about their sexual exploits, and there is absolutely no filter on what comes out of their mouths. I saw a pattern of openly trying to discredit others in any way possible. Deny it all you want, but social media has opened a gateway for anything goes. My cracked foundation was starting to crumble even more.

While I have been teased over years about glasses or having a lazy eye, I do not think I had ever been disliked for trying to better myself. And I sure did not expect it from work peers who were older than me. And there was one who just outright hated me, and they were a self-proclaimed Christian. I would be exhausted from school and studying, and then I would have to go to work with someone whose sole mission was to make my life awful. I tried being nice. I tried to ignore the snide comments. I would sit outside for eight of the twenty-four hours of my shift and would wait until they left to go back inside. I tried doing nice things for them but to no avail. They hated my very presence and wanted me gone. Love your neighbor and turn the other cheek was getting harder and harder. By then we were not in church, and I was not praying or studying God's Word regularly. But I kept thinking it would get better, and I really had a desire to serve the people in my area. Somehow, I made it through paramedic school at the top of my class, with a lot of studying. My son and I graduated and walked the stage together. It was and still is a very precious moment. He worked in a different area than I did, and I stayed where I was. I thought getting my medic license would make things easier, but it did not. Trust me, if you do not heed those words in verse 15, I can promise you lives will be destroyed.

Have you ever been the victim of someone's hatred of you?

Have you ever just taken something over and over, because you were trying to honor God?

Have you been bullied by other Christians? If so, how did you handle it?

How can we reach the younger generations, when the things of the world are seemingly more attractive?

Unfortunately, at the time I was going through this, I was not handling it well at all.

DAY 7

A Sensitive Soul in a Jaded World

*Having lost all sensitivity, they have given themselves
over to sensuality so as to indulge in every kind of
impurity, with a continual lust for more.*
—Ephesians 4:19 NIV

I can admit with certainty, I will never understand the ways of God. All I know is He created in me a sensitive soul. Sometimes I just sit and look up at the heavens and ask, *Why did You give me a sensitive spirit, when I have had to endure so much emotional and physical trauma in my life?* The only answer that ever enters my mind is somebody must be sensitive to others' needs.

I will tell you firsthand. Since 2017, I have not wanted this gift from God. And it is a spiritual gift to be empathic to others. It is a gift to be compassionate. It is a gift to try to love others who live unrighteous lives. Only God can help you love the unlovable. I have over the years tried my best to treat people like I wanted to be treated. I think it is because of how I was treated growing up. Some say physical abuse is worse than mental abuse. But since I have been a victim of both, I can tell you mental abuse is worse. There is nothing worse than someone getting inside your head and filling it with negativity.

I had gone to great lengths over the years to distance myself from negative people, but somehow, I found myself right in the middle of people's negativity and bitterness. That old saying that you become what you are surrounded by is very true. I found myself doubting myself. I was letting the negativity and constant bullying to start creeping into my mind. I was slowly drowning in a cesspool of spiritual emptiness. I lived in a world of jealousy, hatred, bullying, and a lack of any kind of leadership. And my heart was starting to harden like the people around me. If you read verse 18 of Ephesians 4, it talks about the hardening of hearts. In Greek, *harden* literally means petrified. I have a petrified wood collection, and that is some hard rock. So in a sense, my heart was turning into rock. All I can think now is why would anyone want their heart morphed into rock?

I could feel myself becoming calloused and unfeeling. I was numb on the inside, and it was spilling over into my personal life. I was shoving all the people I loved away. I was withdrawing into a dark abyss of utter chaos. Looking back, I was trying to cope by shutting the caring, compassionate side of me off. I did not want to feel anything! But I felt everything around me, and it was a constant tug-of-war between wanting to be compassionate and kind and feeling jaded and angry. Without a church home and godly accountability, things just kept spiraling out of control, until I did not even recognize myself anymore. I could put on a smile, and to the outside world, things looked good. Even my truest friends did not recognize the turmoil in my life. But my husband did, and even he would eventually not be able to stop the train wreck that was coming. I will share his thoughts on the matter.

> You allowed all the negativity from the classmates, coworkers, and the leadership to consume you, to the point that there was very little left of the girl that climbed in my truck window twenty-five years before.

How sad is that statement? He could see all that was happening and was desperately trying to rescue me from myself. But I was stubborn and wanted to serve in my area. The irony of it all, I loved my patients, and they loved me. Why? Because God still wanted me to have empathy and compassion. I thank Him every day that He did not and has not given up on me. And I am thankful my husband did not leave me but stood by my side. I remember that day as well. It has been thirty years now since I jumped up in that window and told him he had the prettiest eyes I had ever seen. The years between 2017 and 2022 have certainly hurt us, changed us, and hopefully made us stronger together.

In such a jaded and calloused world, how do you cope, especially if you are a sensitive soul like me?

Do you retreat inside of yourself? Do you get your feelings hurt and stop doing God's work?

Is your heart becoming petrified? If so, think of some biblical applications to change the hardening of your heart.

I have learned that some people enjoy seeing you in misery because they are miserable. Ask God to give you discernment when to walk away from people filled with negativity and bitterness. You are not the Savior—Christ is. Let Him move you where you need to be.

DAY 8

Under the Wrong Leadership

Hezekiah trusted in the Lord, the God of Israel. There was no one like him among all the kings of Judah, either before him or after him.
—2 Kings 18:5 NIV

All throughout the Bible, we see good leaders, and we see bad leaders. I would suggest you read all of chapter 18 in 2 Kings to know the full story of Hezekiah. Hezekiah chose to do right before the Lord, while others openly disobeyed God. Disobedience comes with a price, as does obedience. It is easy to do wrong, but it is harder to do the right thing. Doing the right thing will cost you friends and family. The one thing I have learned following the crowd has always been easy. You are indulging in mutual things whether good or bad. When you stop following the crowd of wrongdoing, you immediately lose those people. Everybody doing wrong wants to be around others doing wrong, because then their sin does not look bad.

I had an employer one time tell me that he wanted his book-work aboveboard no matter how much complaining he did. I kept them to the penny, and yes, there were times we butted heads, but in the end the right thing was always done. I became used to honest conversations, and I appreciated the fact that he trusted me and my work. That is why I was unprepared for a passive leadership. I was caught very off guard and should have listened to people who had been there before me. And I should have listened to my husband, but hindsight is twenty-twenty.

I was seeing things that were in not so black and white and was being treated like a complete outcast. I begged the owners to please stop the constant bullying and harassment. Their answer was always "We will investigate it" or "Well, we did not see it happen." Long story short, nothing was ever done. Being we were friends and had each grown in Christ in the same church, I was shocked and hurt that they thought so little of me. And even more hurt that they would even insinuate that I was untruthful. I can say that I learned the art of documentation so I would not lose my license. Unfortunately, things just kept getting worse, and things escalated into a physical altercation between me and one other. It is something that I am not proud of at all. But I also know that under correct leadership, it would not have happened at all. You cannot straddle the fence in life. You must pick a side. Either you pick right or you pick wrong. Just like all the kings in the Bible, they had a choice of picking right or wrong. Some did right, and some did wrong, and we are the same way.

As Christians, we are supposed to strive to do the right things, even if it makes us unpopular. During this time, I slipped many times over onto the wrong side of the fence, and I am so ashamed of the person I was at that time in my life. We will discuss the complete demise over the next couple of days. Yes, it gets worse.

But today, I would like for you to look at what side of the fence you are on. Is it for the good or for the bad?

Do you think there is such a thing as staying neutral, by straddling the fence? Give a rationale behind whatever answer you pick.

Do you put your trust in God or "godly" friends? Bear in mind that each of us falls short of the glory of God. We all sin, but if you habitually do the same thing over and over, that is a problem. I am working on one of mine as I write this. I will be honest: it is the things that can come out of my mouth.

How can we learn from Hezekiah, who by the way was only twenty-five when he became king? What made him a good leader? And if you read about other kings, why did they fail?

I have learned that I would rather have true, honest friends who practice what they say, teach, or preach about God. There are enough faux Christians in the world, so let us strive to be as genuine as we can in Christ by practicing His teachings. Talk is cheap, but following through with godly actions is golden.

DAY 9

When Momma Came to Town

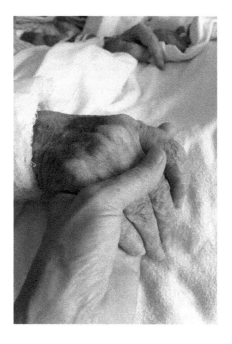

*Honor your father and your mother, so that you may live
long in the land the Lord your God is giving you.*
—Exodus 20:12 NIV

This scripture is the hardest in the Bible for me to read and accept. I
have had many discussions with a pastor about my mother. As I have

mentioned, she was extremely bipolar. And every time I read this passage, I cringed. Then I would feel guilty for not wanting a lot of communication with her. I finally realized that I could limit my contact with her if she was in a destructive state. That may seem harsh to the ones who have a wonderful relationship with their mother, but I did not have that type of relationship with my mother. I cherish the days when she was good and played the piano and sang with others in churches. She was a child prodigy and had an extraordinary talent on the piano. She could play by sight reading and by ear and could take a piece of music and make it even better. But the depressive days were horrific, and no amount of medication ever seemed to work.

Then one day, I had to go get her due to declining health, and I had not spoken with her for four years. Her choice, not mine, but she could no longer live on her own. She had early dementia, had COPD, and was legally blind. Not to mention she had to be on oxygen 24/7. After getting power of attorney, my children went and picked her up from the hospital Christmas Eve in 2018. I had to put her in a nursing home close to me so I could make sure she was taken care of. She had to have all new clothes, and it took one month to get her hair back to some semblance of normal. I did not know the last time it had been washed; she had just been putting dry shampoo in it. And yes, someone was living with her "supposedly" taking care of her; but unfortunately, she was just being taken advantage of. Along with her being bipolar, she was very OCD about her appearance and house. It was a good thing that she could not see how bad the house looked or herself, for that matter.

It was very hard for me to take on the responsibility of being her caretaker due to the feelings of resentment of her not taking care of me like a mother should. But the commandment in Exodus was always in my mind. For one year, I would go to the nursing home just about every day and make sure she had snacks and her necessities. I did her laundry, decorated her room with some of her things, and tried to make it comfortable for her. She had a wonderful roommate, which gave her someone to talk to. I even got her to start playing the piano there. She had not played in over two years, but even being mostly blind, her fingers still remembered where to go. We had good days and bad. I can say her dementia made her more likable and funnier. She still had days that she was extremely difficult, but in a way, it gave me some closure. She had gotten some dignity back. For one year, Robby, Zach, and I would check in and run back and forth to make sure all was well. Being a caregiver and working full-time is not easy, and it added stress on me, especially in the environment I worked in. But at the end of the day, I had no regrets for doing the right thing, by honoring a parent. Somewhere inside of me, God was still trying to work on me.

Examine your relationship with your parent. Are you close to your parents? Do you have a difficult parent?

If you have a parent who had mental problems, do you find it hard to obey the commandment in Exodus?

Think of ways that can help you obey the difficult tasks God asks us to do. Sometimes the task is almost more than we ourselves can handle.

For me, it caused suppressed memories to resurface, and they resurfaced when I was at my worst spiritually. I learned some valuable lessons in all the chaos that was hammering me from all sides.

One is you can overload yourself to the point of mental exhaustion. You get so consumed in the task that you forget to take time for yourself and recharge. I should have been in my Bible and praying. Instead, I was going to church sporadically, but I am thankful for the times I went. Looking back, I can see how hard God was trying to soften my heart. But I was going down a path of self-destruction, and the train wreck was about to happen.

DAY 10

The Catalyst That Meant No Harm

Hold on to instruction, do not let it go; guard it well, for it is your life. Do not set foot on the path of the wicked or walk in the way of evil men. Avoid it, do not travel on it; turn from it and go on your way. For they cannot sleep till they do evil; they are robbed of slumber till they make someone fall.
—Proverbs 4:13–16 NIV

This will be a little longer devotion today, so buckle up for a bumpy ride. I have mentioned my son was working for another service, which was a bit of a drive with long hours at a time. I remember vividly when he said he wanted to work for the same service that I did. I immediately said, "No, you do not." It was concerning for me because he is a loner and likes to keep to himself. He just wants to be left alone. I told him there was not much privacy, and I did not want him subjected to the bullying. But he was determined to make the change, and he did. I remember telling the owners that he was very private and did not like to be bothered, especially when you work the hours EMS employees have to work. You need all the rest and quiet time you can get when you work forty-eight hours straight. They said they understood, and for a while things were good, until they were not.

Working in this environment, your partner has to be compatible or things just do not go well. When he was first hired, things were okay. And I enjoyed when we could work together on occasion. He is very confident in his abilities, but you still like to bounce ideas around and talk through difficult calls. Even to this day, we exchange ideas on what may have been better or worse. I have to be very vague on situations as to not violate the Health Insurance Portability and Accountability Act, and I do not want to get into ugly drama either. So I will give general information.

A little background on our relationship: I homeschooled him from the fifth grade up, oddly enough, because of the bullying he endured at school. As a parent, you will go to great lengths to protect your children. And he and I are close because he was with me so much. We had an enjoyable time during those years, and he gained a lot of his confidence back without the constant bullying. He was bullied for being smart. He was bullied because he found a quiet spot to read in the classroom. He was bullied for being good-natured. He was bullied for being different. But we got through all of that, and he became a self-confident young man. But being bullied and berated as an adult is a different ball game altogether.

It is strange to me that someone can dislike you just because you are smart and confident. My viewpoint is that we should encourage and learn from one another. Unfortunately, some people are just not nice. There really is no other way to put it. Sometimes in life, situations are recognizable in an instant; and then other situations start so gradual, you do not see them coming. This was the case with me and then with my son. I was so beaten down by this point, I did not see the obvious signs he was presenting with. Slowly his attitude changed; he became more irritable, and he started losing hair. I felt helpless because I was watching a happy-go-lucky young man starting to become the opposite of who he was. I asked him to tell me, when I started writing about the devotion today, how he felt at the time. He thought about it for two days, and he sent this to me:

> I had a feeling of being trapped and depressed all the time.

It is amazing how one or two people can try to destroy someone else. And what is worse, he tried several times to discuss the situation with the owners, but he was told the exact same thing I was. They did not see it, so there was nothing they could do. It finally escalated to the point that he had to get out of a situation, before it turned even more ugly than it already was. I will not discuss the event, but I will say that looking back at how he had to handle it, it was the best decision he could make at the time.

This took place on a Sunday, and that was the last day either of us would ever have to stay in that colossal mess again. It was also the day we lost people that we had shared many wonderful moments with. It was a day that, in my mind, evil took center stage. Satan can take a hold of anything when you are not clothing yourself in God's armor. I can unequivocally say we were unprepared spiritually or mentally at this point in our lives to handle the barrage of attacks by Satan. And he was not through attacking either. Tomorrow's devotional will focus on the fallout of all the cumulative events that took place over three years. It's not pretty, and for me to revisit that time is like reliving a nightmare.

If you are having a season of despair and feel like Satan is wreaking havoc in your life, please read Ephesians 6:10–20. I wish I had read that repeatedly.

Ask yourself if you believe 100 percent in this scripture. If you feel weak or struggle in your faith, please read verse 18 over and over again. Scream it out if you need to. But do not allow Satan into tricking you that when you pray, God is not listening.

How often do you pray and put on the armor of God?

How has Satan used people to undermine your beliefs?

Have you ever had to watch your children go through things and you thought there was nothing you could do?

Do you believe evil can intrude in your mind, your family, and your friends?

The two passages of Scriptures referenced today both talk about evil. One tells us people cannot sleep until they inflict evil on someone. The other one tells us to put on the full armor of God so you will be ready when evil comes your way.

I know from personal experience that without God's Word, without praying over everything and suppressing the Holy Spirit, evil will find the cracks in your armor. And it will latch on to you like a parasite, and the only antidote is God. And you will have battle scars to remind you that without God, you can be destroyed mentally, physically, and spiritually.

DAY 11

The Day I Chose to Die

I say to God my Rock, "Why have you forgotten me? Why
must I go around mourning, oppressed by the enemy?"
My bones suffer mortal agony as my foes taunt me.
Saying to me all day long "Where is your God?"
—Psalm 42:9–10 NIV

January 13, 2020, is a day I barely remember, but a day I will never forget. I remember standing in the kitchen, wondering how my life was spinning so out of control. It was one thing for me to endure the bullying and harassment, but when things escalated with my son

30

having to get out of a hostile situation, something snapped in my brain. He was being harassed, and at the same time he was being blamed for removing himself from the situation. I absolutely could not understand how people whom I loved could betray us so harshly. It made me feel like I was an outcast.

I remember looking at Robby's insulin, thinking to myself, *The world is better off without you.* I wrote a letter to Robby, and then I grabbed his insulin pen and just started injecting myself with insulin. I just wanted the pain and bullying to stop. I know I had talked to Robby that day, but my brain had gone so haywire, I did not even know I had texted him and told him what I had done. In my mind, I thought he had called me right after I did it. I know God intervened profoundly that day. Somehow in a daze, my two dogs and I wandered around in the woods and crossed a creek, and the next thing I remember is waking up in an ambulance and seeing Robby. All I could think was *Why did you do it?* I remember bits and pieces of the ER and being sent to ICU and nothing until the next day.

Before I talk more about that day, I am going to share some things I had started writing in 2018 and 2019, when the harassment was getting worse and worse. To answer the question I know you may have, I to this day do not know why I did not remove myself from the situation. I just know that I desperately wanted to serve in my county. I am stubborn to a fault, and I was not letting God lead. It is painful for me to read and share the words I had been writing, but they tell of how out of control I was. I thought I had destroyed some of the writings, but I found some I had kept in a book. I will share some excerpts from different dates all addressed to Robby. So here goes.

September 16, 2018

There are no words to explain how I feel. I wish there were, but not wanting to live is like a disease.

I have given up on people and their integrity. It seems there is no end in this awful cycle.

I feel isolated and alone most of the time. People see what they want to see, but they never try and go beyond the superficial. The church as a whole does not reach out and try to help the struggling. Everybody puts on masks, and they pretend all is well.

You have to give me credit I have fought hard the last two years to fit in and try to be accepted, but that is just not working out.

You asked me once why I had to try and be the best? The answer is I was always told I was nothing.

I guess I have tried to prove to myself, I could be good at something.

Look how far I have fallen in the last two years.

I have no fight left in me. Not in my job, church or life.

October 7, 2018

It's an awful feeling to know I have always been people's second or third choice, never anybody's first choice or priority.

March 28, 2019

I feel so small now and trust no one. I sometimes think people just use me for what they can get out of me.

I have been hurt time and time again. Everywhere I turn it seems I just see people that want something from me. I have been used a lot here lately and it hurts so much. I just sit and cry all the time with very few good days.

My spark is gone.

April 2, 2019

I hate myself. And I can't do for everyone anymore.

It is 2023, and rereading these letters makes me sad and angry at the same time. The reason why I chose the scripture from Psalms today is because we all have questioned God. I was so angry with Him during that time. I could not understand why I had fallen so far away from Him. I could not understand how He could allow people to cause so much pain and misery to me and my family.

I know I wrote a couple more in 2019, but I destroyed those. Things just continually got worse over the next few months. My son and I were dealing with bullying, and my mother's health was steadily declining. Taking care of her was emotionally challenging for me. I was trying so hard to work in a bad environment, take care of my mother, and keep my marriage intact all without God's help. My mother passed away in December of 2019, and I thought things would get easier. But Satan was steadily working hard. It was a time to die.

January 13, 2020

I am so sorry, but I cannot go on this way. The last 3 years have just been more than I can bear. I love you too much to have you to suffer with me. But that place and those people are evil.

I never dreamed that people could make you hate the world in this way. But especially by people you thought were your friends.

God made it clear it was not a time to die, but a time to live.

Have you felt this amount of despair?

How do you feel when you think God has abandoned you?

Do you have a strong church family? If not, how can you help in making your church family more aware of people's struggles?

How have you dealt with betrayal from others?

I feel it is important to share Robby's thoughts and memories from that day. Family members can see you spiraling out of control, and it affects them deeply. It is important to have their viewport. Here are Robby's thoughts and memories.

When we spoke that morning, I knew she was very distraught. My thought was, "There is absolutely nothing I can do to fix this." I remember talking at lunch and she was still very upset. I had told her several times over the months prior that she was way too close to the edge. Everything that went wrong was magnified. Again, I was at a place where there was nothing I could do to fix it.

I got her text as I was walking out of the office area into the shop, and it was right after lunch. If it had been any later, the noise would have been so loud that I would have never heard the text go off. It might had been 30 minutes or an hour before I checked my phone. That would have been too late.

I got three miles down the road and decided that I needed to call a paramedic and get him down there to try and find her, since I knew she had taken my insulin. I was not really panicking that much because I knew there was some amount of time left, and I was focused on trying to fix it. This I could fix!

By the time I got home there were several deputies there and the paramedic had just finished checking the house, so I went down to the creek, and we found her phone on the ground. I knew we were on the right track. I sent some North to that line and sent some East. I told them to look for the dog, because she would be close to her. Find the dog and she would lead the way.

I made a large loop North and then East and had made it to the power line when someone yelled out that they found the dog. Maybe a minute later they found her leaning against a tree with both dogs with her. One of the deputies said that she was still breathing, so I knew for sure we could get her back.

When she did come to, she was angry and I am sure she was going through a flood of emotions, as she came back to her senses. I did not want any outside stimulation for the near future, so I told the EMT not to let anyone come up to the hospital checking on her. The time was too late for concern.

The next days and weeks were spent letting everything sink in and trying to put the pieces back together.

One thing I have learned from this experience was that once a person or object is broken, both can be put back together. They will never be quite the same, whether in appearance or strength. You can never unbreak anything. If you glue something back together, it takes a certain amount of time to cure and be made strong again. That is non-negotiable.

Reading and writing his words literally made me cry. But God has taken our broken pieces and has been molding us back together over the last three years.

I hope you never get to the point I did. But if you find yourself in a similar situation, please reach out to someone. Do not be ashamed to seek counseling. Call the suicide hotline 988. But do not let Satan trick you into thinking you are worthless and that God is not there. Your brain can get sick just like any other part of your body. And never let people tell you it cannot. It can!

DAY 12

The Hospital Stay

*In the same way, the Spirit helps us in our weakness. We do
not know what we ought to pray for, but the Spirit himself
intercedes for us with groans that words cannot express.*
—Romans 8:26 NIV

Waking up in an ICU bed the day after I had attempted to take my
on life was scary in so many ways. I could not look at anyone, nor did
I want to talk to anyone. All I could think was why I did it and how
stupid I was. And to make things worse, someone had to sit with me
day and night. I had no privacy to process what I did, much less talk
to God. But this verse speaks volumes to me. I have the Holy Spirit
who can translate my groans.

Robby was able to sit with me some, and I had two people who
came and brought me a trauma llama and another who brought me
encouraging books to read. Even though they did not understand the
why, they demonstrated they cared. I am thankful for that. It was
hard to face people because I was so ashamed of what I had done.
But at the same time, I was exasperated with all that I had had to
deal with. It felt like I had two different thought processes going on
in my mind. One was just wanting to curl up in a ball and give up,
and the other was wanting to live wholly again. At the time, I had no
idea which thought would win.

I will say most everyone was nice, but one woman who would visit was only making things worse. I really do not know what her position was in the hospital, but it had something to do with follow-up rehab. She kept telling me what I was going to do, but she never asked me what had happened or how I wound up in the condition I was in. She kept wanting to ship me off somewhere. But she told me I needed church and God, and her church was the place to go. I almost hollered at her. Somewhere I found the restraint to keep my mouth shut. The last thing I needed for her was to think I was hostile. She never once asked me my relationship with God; she just assumed that if I had had a relationship with God, I would not be where I was. The last words I wrote in yesterday's devotion was that your brain can get sick. It is part of the same body that can get the flu, cancer, COVID, or any other disease. I wanted to tell her that I prayed, I shouted out to God, I begged to God, and I was a believer. The downfall was that I had not listened to God when He was trying to nudge me away from the situation I was in.

After about three days, I got a wonderful doctor who actually listened to me. She asked me how I was feeling, and she wanted my input on the best treatment for me. I told her I wanted to go home and do outpatient therapy. She told me there was no hold on me to have to stay and that she would get me set up with outpatient therapy. The woman I had been dealing with was agitated with the therapy I had chosen, and I never saw her again. It made me realize that we have a serious problem on how to best treat our mental health issues in our country. I had never had any until the situation I had endured, but I had seen my mother's treatments never worked for her. Sometimes as Christians, we do not want to believe or help when people have mental health issues. I think the reason we cannot relate is because we cannot see it physically, and we may have not had to endure trauma that can cause PTSD. But do not ever try to shame someone because you think they do not believe in God.

Do you have a family member who struggles with any mental disorder? If so, how do you deal with them?

Do you avoid them? Do you help them?

When you have church members who struggle, how do you interact with them?

Does your church help in a godly way people who have an acute or chronic mental health issue?

From experience in dealing with someone with a chronic mental disorder, it is difficult and challenging to be there 24/7. I have learned when I can help and when I need to step back. I have learned how to pray more specifically on some disorders. The brain is so misunderstood, and some are born with disorders that treatment never helps. My brain suffered from constant mental abuse, but I have found a treatment that works.

Pray that you can help when needed. Pray that the church helps when needed. But understand that sometimes a mental disorder may never be healed just like any other disease. Jesus says we should love all, even when they are unlovable. And sometimes we must back away and let someone else minister for a while.

DAY 13

Coming Home to Heal

He heals the brokenhearted and binds up their wounds.
—Psalm 147:3 NIV

It is better to take refuge in the Lord than to trust in humans.
—Psalm 118:8 NIV

The day I came home, I had no job, very little hope, and absolutely no trust left for people. I was utterly and completely broken. I wanted to be by myself. I did not even want Robby around. The first few days were surreal. I had walked into my own home, but I felt out of place. I felt like an empty shell with nothing left to offer. I could tell my son was feeling some of the hurt I was feeling as well. He literally stayed in his room or to himself for almost a month. There were three people living in a house with little to no communication.

I did not know how to move forward. It is strange, but I could not even cry. I was angry with myself and angry with people. I was just going through the motions of life. I did not want to leave my home and go anywhere. I did not want to watch TV, ride a horse, or even walk the creek. I would wake up screaming from nightmares many a night. Loud noises made me jump. My anxiety attacks were brutal. PTSD is a very real thing, and it can be triggered by the most minute thing. I also knew the rumors that were floating around. People meant well when they would send a message about the things people were saying, but it just added more hurt on top of the hurt that was already there. And there were a lot of false things being said, because people are never the villain in their own recount of events. But that is neither here nor there. I definitely could have done some things differently. So how do you start to heal?

For me, there was not a single incident, but rather a nudge here and there from ones whom I could semitrust. That is why I chose two scriptures for today. Both tell you where your refuge is. We can seek His refuge for healing. I am not saying it is an easy fix by any means. Believe me when I say I was not trusting God like I should have been. I do not want to lead people into believing that by trusting in the Lord your life will be perfect. I want you to know that the closer you draw to Him, the easier the burden is to bear. Life will never be perfect, but it is a comforting feeling knowing He is there. I am writing these words three years after my suicide attempt. So do not be misled into thinking my healing was overnight either. It has been a long process.

Other than going to my first outpatient therapy session, I had not gone anywhere. January 31, 2020, I was convinced by my son and his friends to go bowling. It was my first time getting back out in the world. Robby and I both enjoyed getting out and laughing with them. It was a start, and there would be several more baby steps along the way. Then another friend convinced us to go be extras in a movie that was being filmed in our state. It was a fun distraction, especially since we did not know anybody else. I did not have to worry about the judgmental looks from anyone. After that, I was able to be with a friend and his family when he got his heart transplant. Looking back, I can see that God was allowing me to do things away from my hometown. He gave me opportunities to slowly start putting my life back together. At the time, I was still too blinded by anger and hurt to see Him working. During that time, a disease named COVID was starting to creep into our lives, and isolation was about to set in. This time was hard on many people, but for me, it was a blessing and a curse. It allowed me to have the solitude I needed to draw closer to God and to find myself again.

In your darkest hours, do you believe that God is our refuge? Why or why not?

Sometimes when we think about wounds, we think of a visible wound. But wounds are external and internal. When you are broken on the inside, is it more difficult for you to cry out to God?

Where do you put your trust and faith? People or God?

When a trust is broken from a fellow believer, do you blame God, or do you try to trust Him more?

I wish I could say that I put all my faith and trust in God during this time, but I was just hurting so deep internally that I felt numb. But, friend, God can and will take that pain and start turning it into good. It may not be in the way you want it to be, but be patient. I am unsure a lot of days of His will and where He wants me, but I am feeling more confident in some areas of my life. I still and will always need continual direction.

DAY 14

Soul-Searching in the Spring and Summer

*I remember my affliction and my wandering, the bitterness
and the gall. I well remember them, and my soul is downcast
within me. Yet this I call to mind and therefore I have hope:
Because of the Lord's great love we are not consumed,
for his compassions never fail. They are new every
morning; great is your faithfulness.*
—Lamentations 3:19–23 NIV

These verses Jeremiah wrote are a beautiful reminder of God's faithfulness. As mentioned yesterday, COVID was rearing its ugly head in the spring of 2020. I was not working at that time, so I spent a lot of time alone. But I needed the isolation to come to terms with what I had done and how I got to that point of utter hopelessness. I started walking all over the woods, the creek, and the streets of my little community. I had very little contact with anyone, but I was crying out to God every day. As I was walking, I saw the rebirth of the trees and flowers. I watched barren trees start budding with new green foliage. I saw flowers sprouting up from the decaying matter on what was left over from the winter. It was a time of renewal and a lot of soul-searching.

We have horses, and our first foal was born that April on a Sunday. Our very first foal born on the property, and she came on a Sunday. I do not think that was by chance that she was born on the Lord's day. That sweet little filly brought pure joy to my heart. Looking back, I can see where God was helping my heart to feel something other than bitterness and regret. I enjoyed walking out there every day and loving on sweet little Olive Bell. Slowly, I was starting to enjoy parts of life again.

I planted a garden, I picked berries for jelly, and I roamed the property quite often. I started searching the creek again for arrowheads and fossils. I was trying desperately to rise up from the pain and brokenness. My emotions were so raw and so fragile. I called my grandmother often during this time. We talked about gardening, canning, and making pickles. She had turned ninety that January, and I had to miss her birthday party, which I felt terrible about. At that time, no one outside of my immediate family knew what had happened. I finally told her and talked to her about it. I remember distinctly what she told me, "Dawn, I never went through anything like that, as I did not work much outside the home. And I am so sorry that you had to go through that." She told me she loved me, and we continued talking a lot throughout the summer. It was so comforting to me to talk about gardening, recipes, and our love of flowers.

Robby and I had started going back to the church where we got married. It just felt right at the time. It had been a while, and we could both just sit and worship. He was not leading music, and I did not worry about being the wife of the music minister. Church was outside for a while, and then it went to wearing a mask and sitting at a distance. We sat in the back and enjoyed the services and even started singing duets together again. It was nothing formal, and it was fun without any pressure. God kept His church going throughout the pandemic, as He has for centuries.

That spring and summer, God was allowing me to be rejuvenated. Slowly the nightmares were going away, but I was still hanging on to a lot of anger and resentment. The anxiety attacks I could control some with medication, but they were still frequent when I would leave the house. I often wonder what God thinks when He is trying so hard to keep us on the right path, and we just continually wander off in another direction. He is so faithful, and we are so rebellious. And He was guiding us in a direction that neither Robby nor I saw coming.

How do you communicate with God when life seems hopeless?

Do you see God's faithfulness working in the midst of chaos?

Do you need people around you, or do you need solitude in times of despair?

I needed the solitude due to my hurt from people. I needed to learn how to trust people again. I needed simplicity so my brain could heal. Ask God what you need. When I cried out to Him, I had no idea how He was going to start the healing process. But He gave me the quietness and the solitude to be renewed and refreshed. He showed me the people I needed at that time. He removed people from my life as well. He was my sanctuary in my time of trouble. The Holy Spirit will guide you, if you allow it. Remember, you have to have the faith that He will guide you through your turmoil, and that is hard sometimes.

DAY 15

Trusting in the Unknown

*Do nothing out of selfish ambition or vain conceit, but in humility
consider others better than ourselves. Each of you should look not
only to your own interests, but also to the interests of others.*
—Philippians 2:3–4 NIV

Two very distinct things happened almost simultaneously in the fall of 2020. My son told me there was an opening with the company he was working for. Now I was hesitant and did not want to have another bad experience with work partners. My counselor was wise when she told me I needed time to heal or I would bolt if I got back into the same situation I had been in. My son assured me the place and the one I would be working with would be good. He would know because he had been through some of what I had gone through. After praying and discussing the matter with Robby, I decided to give it a go. I always loved the patients I had contact with, because it was an opportunity to help, talk, and learn about people. When you are in the back of an ambulance with people, you are putting patients' interests first whether it is a big emergency, transfer, or sometimes not an emergency. I do love to talk with people, and there are some pretty interesting conversations that can go on in the back of the ambulance. I have laughed, prayed, and cried with people many a day. I have all kinds of patients, and I can say that all were treated with respect from me, even some who did not deserve it. But you can de-escalate a situation very quickly by being humble and kind.

Even though I was scared to go back to work, I felt I had to trust that God was opening that door. I certainly was not looking. It was just what I needed at the time. The station I was at was quiet in the manner that it was just you and your partner. I had a good partner, and we got along well. I gained a lot of my confidence back, and I needed that. I was blessed that both EMTs I worked with there were terrific. We functioned well as a team. When you love the job, you need people who work well together.

The second opportunity was a church where Robby had previously served asked him to come back as the minister of music. It was very unexpected, and he wanted to say no, but the one who called told him, "Before you answer, please just pray on it." We both were so shocked because we had wandered so far away from God. But God was always there gently trying to pull us back into the fold. Robby agreed to meet with the committee. As mentioned in day 5, he explained to them the emotional toil we had been through. He asked them politely not to put any pressure on me for anything. He knew how bad my anxiety was, but we both knew God was wanting us back in church full-time. We definitely did not have any self-ambitions. We were both so broken. I was so downcast and ashamed of myself; I could barely look up in the services. Slowly, the Holy Spirit was chipping away at my petrified heart. He was whispering to me that I still had something left to offer. He put us where we needed to be, and He knew we were imperfect, struggling people. We both had a lot of anger and mistrust. We were struggling as well trying to heal our marriage. I consider this time in our lives was the start of a healing process. God gave me an opportunity to gain confidence back in my job. God put Robby back in his ministry. These are both things that came unexpectedly, but we knew they were a God thing. It was not easy going back into either. Neither of us were conceited or vain, but we were selfish in the fact that we did not want to interact with people outside of a few friends. Somehow, we had to find a way to regain trust and learn how to minister to others again.

Do you serve when God calls you?

Do you try to serve to please yourself or God?

Have you ever been conceited in your ministry or job?

Do you envy others when it seems that their walk with God is better than yours?

I can say I have never been conceited because I have always lacked self-confidence. I have gained confidence in some aspects of my life, but I still let people make me feel small. That is something that I may always feel, but after what I went through, God showed me that I am valuable to Him. I know people think that if I was valuable to Him, why did I get to that point of desperation?

Because I was not living my life in tune with God. I had turned away from Him. I can own that. I know my mistakes all too well. It has taken me three years to fully admit that I had turned my back on Him. Am I at the place I was years ago? No, but I am getting there and with a lot more experience of knowing when Satan is taking aim at me. So be humble and compassionate toward others, but as mentioned before, know when to step back and recognize when evil rears its ugly head. Let God handle the big and small things in your life.

DAY 16

Mental Health and the Church

Be joyful in hope, patient in affliction, faithful in prayer. Share with God's people who are in need. Practice hospitality.
—Romans 12:12–13 NIV

I will probably ruffle some feathers on the matter of mental health and the church. I believe they need to be ruffled. Nowhere in the Bible does it reference mental health directly. It references demons in Matthew 10:8 and in various other scriptures. Before anyone thinks that I do not believe in angels or demons, I do. The Bible states both exist. But somewhere along the line, I believe some thought that true mental illness was because someone had a demon. As I mentioned before, the brain can and will get sick. But if you look back over time, there were some severe methods to rid one's "demon." Exorcisms, electric shock therapy, and lobotomies were a few methods used to heal a mental disorder. Some died, and some made worse than they were before, but they were still performed. The church as a whole is not so great with helping people with a mental disorder. People tend to shy away from something they do not understand. And even going through the experience I had, I still do not understand fully the depth of chronic mental illness. I can only explain what it is like for your coping mechanism to break.

I can, however, tell you that my mother was very well versed in the Bible. She knew the Scripture. She knew and believed in God, but she was never cured from being bipolar and other mental disorders. She was placed in an institution twice and was on various medications throughout her lifetime. It may have helped some, but she still had terrible moments. She, like Paul, had a thorn in her flesh; and it was never taken away here on earth. Who better than Paul to write those verses listed above? I would encourage you to read 2 Corinthians 11:22–27. Paul knew all types of afflictions, and one was never removed after pleading with the Lord three times to remove it (2 Corinthians 12:8).

Yesterday's devotion talked about God's help for us to start healing, but He also knew I needed help from a doctor. I got outpatient therapy and the right medication, and I needed it. When you ask God for help, it can come from both the spiritual and the earthly realm. I ask that we as a church quit demeaning someone's mental health and start understanding it is a disease. Can God take away diseases of all sorts? Of course, He can, but does everyone get healed?

No! Remember we live in a fallen world. I would like to think that we can agree that we should practice those verses of scripture above.

Three years later, I still go to see my therapist. I continue to go not because I am in a dark place; I go because I can share things and get an unbiased answer. She is someone that I can converse freely with. There are some things that your family or friends cannot help you with. They may be too close to the situation, or they may have never experienced what you are going through. So there is no shame in seeking counseling.

I could have placed this devotional topic anywhere in this book, but I wanted you to know the problem first and how I started my healing. I say that because I wonder if I would have had the same outcome if I had been in church regularly. I cannot answer that question, partly because I have seen firsthand how Christians have handled situations like mine. I have seen how they have treated others who have struggled with PTSD, addiction, or a chronic mental disorder. People like for things to look perfect. But nothing is perfect, absolutely nothing. Life is complicated and messy.

What do you like to see when you walk through the church doors on Sunday morning regarding people? What should the church look like to others?

How do you feel about the way mental health has been dealt with in the past?

Do you believe that God and medicine can work together?

I can tell what my perspective is on what a church should look like. It should have mature Christians, new Christians, and unsaved people. It should feel like a sanctuary, not a country club. I have walked into churches knowing people who have all sorts of problems, but that happy mask is in place. People will not reach out for help if they believe the church is only for perfect people. There have been times when I wanted to go to the altar and cry my eyes out, but all that goes through my mind is what will people think? I am trying to change my mindset on that, because the only one I should be focused on is God.

Read Romans 12:16.

DAY 17

The Loss of Friends

Carry each other's burdens, and in this way
you will fulfill the law of Christ.
—Galatians 6:2 NIV

Therefore, as we have the opportunity, let us do good to all people,
especially to those who belong to the family of believers.
—Galatians 6:10 NIV

Be devoted to one another in love. Honor one another above yourselves.
—Romans 12:10 NIV

There are so many scriptures on how to treat each other. I could not pick just one. When I form friendships, I want them to last. I, sadly, have learned that people will avoid you like the plague when things get rough. Somehow, I do not think this is what God intended. We do not help carry each other's burdens, we do not always do good with other believers, and selfishness will not let us honor someone above ourselves. Ouch!

I remember when I started venturing back out into my little town vividly. I had people whom I have helped and talked to for thirty years almost run the other way. People whom I had worked with quit calling or texting. Friends whom I had gone to church with and socialized with cut me off completely. That is a hurt that never truly heals. And I tried reaching out to work things out, but they were taking zero responsibility concerning me. I felt like I had been thrown away like a piece of trash.

I remember walking in the grocery store and seeing someone whom I had talked to fairly often, and they turned their head when they saw me. It made me angry and sad at the same time. This time though I simply said, "You can talk to me. I do not have a disease." They did speak, but it was awkward. I learned that day not to invest too deeply in shallow friendship. I could be nice, but I was going to be wise in whom I put my trust in. That was/is one of the hardest things to do. Why? Because I have always been an outgoing person and loved being around people. Maybe it is because I have always wanted to fit in. When you come from a bad home environment, you want to seek acceptance and belonging from others.

When I moved to where I live now, I was in my early twenties. All the friends I had growing up lived somewhere else. And moving to a place in your adult years makes it hard to find friends. It is not that people are not nice, but they have bonds with people that they have formed from early childhood. So I was grateful for the ones I had formed bonds with. I think that is why the loss was so hard on me. I had trusted my Christian friends with my heart. It broke my heart when some of those people completely shut the door and locked me out of their lives. And other friends would not speak up; they would just tell me how sad it was. And I had stood up for them publicly and privately.

That made my recovery that much harder. It made me where I stayed at home more. When I worked, it was in another area so nobody knew me there. I did not have to worry about what people thought. I got to the point where I lived, I would not go anywhere without Robby. I had only a few people I would talk to or socialize with. I have gone through a wild range of emotions, trying to come to terms with losing people. I realized that I cannot change them or continue to try to reach out. As hard as it is, you must cut ties and move forward. You can forgive people and move on without them.

Have you been hurt by your friends to the point that there is no reconciliation?

How does it feel when you have had shared so much of yourself to other believers and then they reject you?

How do you think God feels when His people hurt one another? How do you think He feels when we hurt Him?

I carried with me so much bitterness and anger inside me for a long time. If left unchecked, it can turn you into the exact opposite of who you want to be. There is no easy fix from hurt by the ones you love. I came to accept how my mother was years ago, so you would think I could overcome this easily. For me, it seems to be harder. My mother had a mental disorder, so I could rationalize how she was. But when you have "normal" people hurt you, it is hard to find an answer to why. The one positive is now if I feel like I have been hurtful to someone in any manner, I will apologize and move on. I do not want to think I may have caused someone unnecessary pain in their life.

DAY 18

Moving Forward Like a Snail

Yet if I speak, my pain is not relieved; and if I refrain,
it does not go away. Surely, O God you have worn me
out, you have devastated my entire household.
—Job 16:6–7 (NIV)

I have told you several tools that God was using in my healing process, but healing is hard. You have good days and horrible days. These words from Job are exactly how I felt a lot of days. I was exhausted and tired of the same memories recurring all the time. I wanted to pack those memories away in my brain. But everywhere I went in my community, there were constant reminders. Robby and I were still walking on eggshells around each other. But there were still positive things happening.

The summer of 2020, my son and I were sitting outside, and I knew he was still miserable with his job. He liked a lot of things about his job, but it was not what he originally wanted to do. The experience he and I had shared did not help either. But that summer, I told him to start back to school part-time and work on his prerequisites for veterinarian school. That was what he had intended to do to start with. So that fall he started taking classes at a community college. It was a start in the right direction.

Robby and I had started renovating a 1966 Airstream that summer as well. It was fun to decide on colors, fabrics, and the overall layout. Tearing out the unsalvageable parts was therapeutic. We salvaged everything we could and repurposed piping for accent pieces. It took over a year and a half to get her where we could camp. And we still have some minor things left to do. But she has some of her original character, and her broken parts were replaced to make her roadworthy again. Stella Rose came to life again, and now she is bouncing down the road with us and two dogs in tow.

I hope you did not miss the irony here. When I started writing today, I had no idea this comparison was going to unfold. Like Stella Rose, that is just what God was doing to me. He was slowly taking away the broken things in my life and was replacing them with new things. I am not an inanimate object that has no thoughts or feelings. I am a person, and I have felt every broken piece being removed. I have cried over the loss of friends. I have been stubborn with God when I did not think it was fair for me to have and feel so many losses. But every time He removed something, He replaced it with something better. At the time, I could not see that all the changes were making me stronger. He was and still is working on me. He is making me "roadworthy" again. There is no way I could have a productive walk with Him, unless He renewed His spirit in me.

I have by no means experienced the things Job did. And I certainly did not have the mentality Job did when everything fell apart for him. But I can say my pain was real, my household fell apart in a different way, and I was exhausted mentally and physically. It has been a painfully snail-pace process inching my way back into life and building my relationship back with God. I remember how I felt over twenty years ago, when I devoured every morsel I could read or study about God. On the advice of Brother Jim, I went to seminary and got my two-year certificate, through New Orleans Baptist Theological Seminary in biblical teaching. Please understand, I had a very personal and intimate relationship with God, and I still fell hard. The reason being I started slacking on my end. I pray that the road back to Him makes me stronger and wiser going forward.

Have you ever had a Job moment in your life? If so, how did you react to it?

If you have not fully read or studied Job, I encourage you to do so. And then ask yourself, are you like Job, his friends, or his wife?

Have you let God remove your broken pieces so you can be reshaped and rejuvenated better than before?

I prayed many days for God to allow me to minister to others. And He has. I have taught, I have served on the mission field, and I have served Him through music. And then it was gone during those wilderness years. During this season in my life now, I am singing again and have had mission opportunities that COVID halted for a while. I pray that I can get back on the mission field, and maybe one day I can teach again. I pray that everyone reading this allows God to mold you according to your spiritual gifts.

DAY 19

Long Walks and Long Talks

*And do no grieve the Holy Spirit of God, with whom you
were sealed for the day of redemption. Get rid of all bitterness,
rage and anger, brawling and slander, along with every
form of malice. Be kind and compassionate to one another,
forgiving each other, just as in Christ God forgave you.*
—Ephesians 4:30–32 NIV

My earliest memories are swimming in creeks and rivers, searching for arrowheads, camping, and running wild through the woods. I loved being outside in nature. It was a place to escape from burdens that should never be put on a child. I could daydream about a better homelife, build forts, eat honeysuckle and blackberries, and be a kid for a moment. Those memories of running barefoot laughing and giggling with the sun kissing my face are ingrained in my mind. As a child, I had no idea who I was talking to rambling through the woods. I was just speaking out loud all my hurts and wants. When I came to know the Lord, I knew exactly who I was talking to. So it is of little wonder that when I have problems, I strike out to the woods.

Now I have had all kinds of hurt throughout my life. We all have. But the hurt I was experiencing was on a whole different level. And I did not want to adhere to these verses in Ephesians. I was tired, hurt, and angry a lot. I have walked many a mile over the last three years crying, asking God how people could be so mean, and telling Him I just could not forgive. Sometimes I would walk the roads, and every time I went by the church where my whole family and I were saved, I would regress. I would be thinking, *God, you forged so many good things in this building. How did it all go wrong?* I finally had to quit walking in that direction. I just kept to the woods. To me, an encounter with a snake was better than the memories that would surface going by that church. I walked the creek hunting arrowheads. I would walk down to the creek in the middle of the night when the nightmares would wake me up, and listen to the water spilling over the falls. Some of you may call me crazy, but the things in the woods seemed less dangerous than some human beings. And my dogs took every step I did, so nothing was going to get by them. Every single walk I took and still take, I speak to God audibly. From 2020 to the first of 2022, I would tell Him how I wanted Him to handle this mess. And then I would apologize for having angry thoughts. At the time, I could not see that as He was allowing me to vent, He was slowly absorbing all that hurt and anger.

I have come a long way since all this debacle started, but I still must constantly ask God to help me keep the anger and bitterness away. To be completely honest, the hurt I experienced can still be painfully raw. It is a difficult concept to understand how people can completely turn their backs on you as if you never even existed. As we say today, being ghosted by people we love breaks our heart. But the anger is slowly receding, and I have learned that for me to keep moving forward, I need to forgive my mistakes and their mistakes. Some days the process of healing is easy and some days hard. I have had to find ways to redirect my thoughts and energy. I also had to face the reality that some people may never be a part of my life again. There are some that I am glad are not a part of my life now. You can forgive people, but at the same time, you may have to stay away from them.

How have you handled painful losses in life?

Do you keep chasing after people even when you know the outcome will be disastrous?

Can you take a step back and just let God handle the situation, even if you do not think the punishment fits the crime?

Matthew 7:2 says,

> For the same way you judge others, you will
> be judged, and with the measure you use, it will
> be measured to you.

This verse keeps me in my place. I do not want to be measured by some of the things that can go through my mind. I may think or say something, and then I immediately tell God, "I am sorry." At some point, you need to start letting God take away all the hurt, bitterness, and anger you may feel about someone. Will you be the same? No. I have to look at what I went through as a learning lesson of knowing when to walk away before the disaster happens.

DAY 20

Setbacks Will Happen

Create in me a pure heart, O God, and renew a steadfast
spirit within me. Do not cast me from your presence or take
your Holy Spirit from me. Restore to me the joy of your
salvation and grant me a willing spirit, to sustain me.
—Psalm 51:10–12 NIV

I rise before dawn and cry and cry for help;
I have put my hope in your word.
—Psalm 119:147 NIV

David's plea in Psalm 51 begging mercy and forgiveness is something every single believer has done. The psalmist in chapter 119 shares with us that our first thought of the day should be talking to God. This is where I fail most days. I am usually not up before dawn, but when I do get up in the morning, I focus on the things I have to do for the day. I seem to have a problem starting my morning routine with God. I am getting better, but there is room for improvement.

I chose the wilderness Bible today due to all the negative notations I have written in it. I want you to know that none of us are perfect, and we all carry emotional baggage on occasion. In the margins of Psalm 51, I wrote some pretty heavy things down, and I would like to share those thoughts with you.

> I have lost my passion!
> I want to feel again and have a passion again. I need a miracle.
> I do not know how to pray anymore. I feel spiritually, emotionally and Physically dead!
> Why can't I find peace?

Then I picked up the Bible I call the good years and went to Psalm 51. Here is what I wrote in the margin.

> Be humble! Do not put ourselves first rather put God first always.

I had written the answer down on how to handle situations years before I went through the wilderness. Those words were buried so deep inside me that I did not know how to uncover them. I had buried so many beautiful nuggets of God so deep that when I stumble upon them now, I am in awe of how far I had fallen.

I will share of a moment in my healing process that happened about a year ago to illustrate how I need to daily, hourly, and every minute ask for God's help. My hurt was so internal, sometimes I feel like I will never fully recover. And that anger bubbles to the surface every now and then.

Robby and I went to a big barrel run one weekend with several friends, and the first two days went fairly well. I was starting on a new horse, and I guess I thought that going to one of the biggest runs of the year was a good idea. There were around 450 riders there, and this horse had not been exposed to that type of environment. Robby had been riding him some on trail rides, but I had not ridden him much. He was nervous, and I was nervous, but we managed to warm up and make it through the first run at a trot and slow loop coming out. I was not going to push his nerves nor mine. The last day I was riding turned into a disaster. I fell off while trying to mount up in the practice area, because someone popped a whip right by us, and my horse bolted. I am glad I had a helmet on; I ate some dirt. I had changed my reins last minute due to a buckle breaking, and they were a little long and apparently had too much stretch in them. Needless to say, the run was a hot mess. And coming out the gate, somebody just had the unmitigated gall to pop off a smart remark about my reins. I did not even know the person. By then I was madder than a wet old sitting hen in the rain. I got off the horse and just threw my helmet like a fool. Then Robby got mad, and things went even more downhill. I was slinging my stuff around trying to pack it up, and a curse word or two popped out of my mouth. Something spooked the horse while loading him, and he ran back out. By then Robby and I were not speaking to each other, and I am thankful that for some reason, we were in two separate vehicles. He went home, and I just rode around when I got back to the county. I did eventually make it home, and we talked things through later. And please know, no anger was ever directed toward the horse.

Another PTSD moment at its finest. Thankfully, those moments are very rare now. Therapy has worked. Medication has worked. But I cannot stress that by healing my relationship with God, how much more at peace I have become. I am trying to redirect all that bitterness by reading scriptures and having those walks talking out loud to God.

How do you react when things go badly?

Do you meditate on God's Word first thing in the morning?

Can you relate to David in Psalm 51?

I think about that day, and now I can laugh about how stupid I had acted. But I am mature enough to know I will have bad days. Throughout the Bible, there is a constant tug-of-war with good and bad. That is a recurring theme since the fall. We cannot escape bad times, but we can prepare ahead for them. I think some of my anger is directed more to myself, because I had the answer, but I failed to use it. I had let too many secular things occupy my mind. And I failed miserably maintaining my relationship with God. I was putting me first.

DAY 21

Horse Therapy

*Do you give the horse his strength or clothe his neck with a flowing
mane? Do you make him leap like a locust, striking terror with
his proud snorting? He paws fiercely, rejoicing in his strength, and
charges into the fray. He laughs at fear, afraid of nothing; he does
not shy away from the sword. The quiver rattles against his side,
along with the flashing spear and lance. In frenzied excitement he
eats up the ground; he cannot stand still when the trumpet sounds.
At the blast of the trumpet he snorts, "Aha!" He catches the scent
of battle from afar, the shout of commanders and the battle cry.*
—Job 39:19–25 NIV

To me there is nothing more beautiful than a horse running free with their tails up and their manes blowing all around. Our baby horses have brought me great joy over the last three years. We were able to watch the mommies give birth and put our hands on a baby foal fresh out of the womb. I blunder around quite often with my camera capturing beautiful horse photography. Each horse has a unique personality, and it amazes me to watch them function as a unit. The mares are moodier and meaner than the geldings. And the stallion thinks he is the most majestic being on the place. He struts around like a peacock. The babies are still trying to find their pecking order in the herd.

I envy the verse where it says, "He laughs at fear, afraid of nothing." I feel as if I have lived in fear most of my life. The fear of my childhood. The fear of never measuring up. The fear of manipulative people. The fear of failing in my marriage. The fear of starting over in my life. It feels like fear and anxiety try to rule my mind. But when I saddle up and feel the horse's movement under saddle and the wind in my hair, it's like my troubles melt away. I feel alive when I am riding. I feel blessed that I have the privilege to be a caretaker to such magnificent creatures. God's description of his creatures is so beautifully illustrated in chapter 39. To me, there is no better way to see beauty of the land than on the back of a horse. And I have seen some beautiful countryside in a lot of states on the back of a horse. I fully believe God allowed those babies to be born on our place at just the right time I would need them. They gave me a purpose and hope of things new. They made me laugh joyfully again. I go out sometimes, and they are basking in the sunshine like a pig in slop, and I will sit down and sing to them or rub their muzzle. They accept me as one of their own.

Horses are not always easy. I have been kicked, bucked off, stepped on, and even rolled by one over the years. Most of the time it was my fault. Sometimes it was just the wrong place at the wrong time. They eat you out of house and home, and then they poop a lot. They have to have pedicures every six weeks. They have to be wormed and vaccinated. And they are prone to having the craziest accidents. It is an everyday commitment to care for them. For me,

I cannot imagine life without them. They gave me a reason to get up and keep going every day. I needed to feel useful. I needed them to occupy my mind with happy thoughts. They were and still are a powerful tool God gave me.

Do you have any kind of animal therapy?

If so, do you feel like it helps when your fears and anxiety are out of control?

When you look at the creation around you, do you notice the beauty that God gave us? Does it make you stand in awe of how remarkable it is?

You may not have horses. You may have dogs, cats, or even chickens; but animal therapy is a proven therapy. There is something very therapeutic grooming a horse or dog. Or maybe just throwing out feed to the chickens. If you can't or don't have pets, find some-thing to give you a purpose every day. It can be something small, but hang on to anything that makes you smile and feel good about yourself. God gives us all kinds of things; we just have to learn how to recognize them when he does. I never dreamed when we bred our mares in 2019 that they would be a beautiful blessing to me in 2020.

DAY 22

Sanctuary at the Creek

The mind of sinful man is death, but the mind
controlled by the Spirit is life and peace.
—Romans 8:6 NIV

Today is January 23, 2023, and once again Satan is trying to disrupt our lives. He has reared his ugly head, and it has caused some hurt feelings within our family. And once again I am looking for the Holy Spirit to guide me.

I have shared many ways that I search for clarity, forgiveness, and strength; and I have alluded to my walking and the creek. But I have not elaborated on all that I do. One of the few fond memories of my father and my childhood was searching for arrowheads. I can say I will hunt for hours for artifacts and fossils. I remember when I finally found a spearhead in my creek, and I was so excited, after looking here and there for years. I have complete solitude, except for a dog splashing around at times. As I have stated over and over, God gives us things at the right time, and I started finding artifacts going through one of the worst times in my life. For the last five years, I have walked that creek in cold, heat, and right after floods. I close my eyes sometimes and just take a big breath and slowly exhale, thanking God for those quiet moments with Him. I feel like that little girl again running around barefoot with the sun kissing her face on those walks. I start dreaming of better days to come and that maybe I could have a little bit of peace. But the things I find makes my imagination run wild.

Every indigenous worked piece I found, I wonder about the person who sat and chipped away at a rock or piece of quartz to make a tool. I wonder about the nomadic lifestyle they led. I have a few pieces that fit my left hand better than my right hand. Was it a man or woman who used the tool? They left absolutely no trace of themselves, except what was made from natural resources. I do not know about their relationship with God, but I find it hard to believe that He did not make Himself known. I do know that when I sit down and listen to nature around me, I feel an overwhelming sense of peace. The trees softly swaying in a slight breeze, the chirping of birds, and the water rippling over the falls are all coming from God's creation. I know someone had to sit before me and hear the same sounds I have heard. It is in those moments I can feel the Holy Spirit working in me. I feel so close to God in the solitude of nature. There are no worldly distractions in those moments. I keep my phone on silent and on the bank. I do not want to be disturbed in those quiet moments. I can feel the Holy Spirit engulfing me in complete tranquility. Sometimes I do not want to walk back up the hill and enter the modern world.

I am sure you can guess that I will be walking that creek today talking with God, asking Him for clarity in a difficult situation once again. My son told me today that I needed a creek walk because listening to the water flowing would help my anxiety in this situation. It is a bit chilly today, but the dogs and I will strike out for one of our adventures and maybe even find an artifact.

Where is your sanctuary when chaos prevails?

Do you like complete solitude so you can communicate with God?

Can you turn your phone off during those times with God?

I know some do not live in a rural setting, where nature is abundant. I have lived in cities with close neighbors. I understand that finding a quiet place can be difficult in some areas. But try! Find your sanctuary, your refuge. I have put my earbuds in and walked with Christian music playing. Maybe you can use earmuffs to block out noise in your home for some quiet time. Go to a local church and ask if you can sit in the sanctuary. I have been in many old churches and just sat and talked to God. And I cannot help but wonder who had been in one of those old churches before me begging God for help. God is always near, but we have to reach out to Him and communicate with Him. It is not a one-way relationship. So please find a place where you can pour your heart out to Him. Psalms 46:1 says,

> God is our refuge and strength, an ever-present help in trouble. (NIV)

The Amplified Bible uses the words *well-proved help*.

DAY 23

Knowing When to Take a Step Back

My soul is weary with sorrow; strengthen me according to your word.
Keep me from deceitful ways; be gracious to me through your law.
—Psalm 119:28–29 NIV

When I went back to work, it was in the height of COVID, and everything was so drastically different. We were wearing mask and body protection, trying not get sick. Everything was being scrubbed down with bleach, and Lysol spray was our new best friend. I felt so sorry for the elderly, because they could not see a face, just a mask. It was a scary time for many. Oddly enough, I never panicked over a COVID patient. I just geared up to protect myself, and then I would spray my shoes and clothes with Lysol. I never got COVID while on the ambulance, and I was in the back with several patients who were positive. I did finally get in working a clinical rotation in the summer of 2022. The only fear I had of it at that point was not bringing it home to my husband, who unfortunately had underlying health issues that made him high risk. Things eventually started getting back to normal, but I was still recovering from the trauma I had experienced. And I had some calls that were hitting to close to home.

Suicide calls at that time just broke my heart. My experience with it would come back, and it was like reliving the nightmare over. The first one, I took a little time off; but after the second one, I knew I needed to step back and reevaluate some things. Watching a grieving family was heartbreaking, and all I could think was that is what my husband and children felt to a degree. So I stepped back to reconcile my thoughts and asked God to strengthen me. As the verse above says, my soul was weary. It needed some more healing.

You may ask why I had to completely step back from work for a while, and the answer is most people in the health care profession make fun of anyone who has emotional trauma. I have heard awful things said about people with suicidal ideations. The number one thing I have heard said is "Why don't they just go on and kill themselves so we do not have to deal with them?" Our mental health problem in the USA is running rampant, and the system is broken. So instead of telling the exact reason for stepping back, I just made myself unavailable. It was the best thing I could do for myself.

By taking a step back, I could breathe and start focusing on myself and God's plan for me. It had been a long time since I let God lead. It was a struggle trying to live according to His Word. I was still standoffish with people at church, because Christian people were the ones who looked the other way when I was bullied and harassed. I was trying to open up, but it was hard. I just sat in the sanctuary during Sunday school and would only engage with a handful of people. I knew though that I had to just sit and listen before I could find a way to communicate with others. Only God could fix that brokenness in me. I needed a fresh word from God. I needed to hear and read His Scripture.

This time has been hard not only with healing, but we were living solely on Robby's income, and it was/is a bit of a struggle. But God has provided for us. I have shot a couple of weddings and other small photo sessions here and there. Creating beautiful memories for people has reawakened a spark inside of me. I have had to sell some things dear to me, but it has been worth it. By following His way, new opportunities were opening up for me. At first, I did not want to walk through those doors because I feared putting myself fully back into the world.

When things in your life get out of control, do you step back or keep trying to trudge through the mess?

When you read the Scripture and pray, do you expect an immediate answer or healing?

God is trying to keep us from deceitful ways. He is telling us that when our soul is weary, go to Him. I wish I could say it is an easy process. But it just is not. I have been on an emotional roller coaster for several years. I wanted to be healed and made whole instantly. But five years of emotional turmoil is not healed easily. It has only been in the last few months that I have really honed in on what God wants from me. I do not make hasty decisions at all. I am like Gideon, throwing out a fleece. I have had to learn to be still and listen, which is difficult. I am terrified I will misinterpret God's will for me. I feel His spirit tugging on my heart about certain areas in my life as I am writing this. I just pray all my decisions are what He wants. I am bone-tired of constantly falling on my face from my own mistakes.

DAY 24

Going Back to School Again

The heart of the discerning acquires knowledge;
the ears of the wise seek it out.
—Proverbs 18:15

I have had an unquenchable thirst for knowledge my whole life. I just love learning new things, and I feel certain that is one thing that will never go away. The first book I can remember being read to me by my grandmother was *The Princess and the Pea*, a Little Golden book. I still love that book. I guess that started my desire to become an avid reader. I have books everywhere in my home. I learned as a child that a book could be an escape from the world. They would take me all over the world, so to speak. They gave me knowledge and longings of things I wanted to do, and knowledge is something no one can take from you. I have studied accounting, photography, biblical teaching, and paramedicine over the years and have worked or had a role in all those professions.

Becoming a paramedic and gaining my associate of applied science was a huge accomplishment to me. Even though I had taken a lot of college classes, I had never obtained a degree. I do have a two-year certificate in biblical teaching that I pray I can use again in some way. I was so excited the day I walked the stage and got my associate's degree. I had such high hopes and dreams of becoming a paramedic. I have covered my experiences of how that turned out. But I still loved the job. An opportunity became available to enroll in a critical care paramedic class, and I remember asking God, "If You want me to take the class, make it clear to me." To me, it felt like I could redeem myself after feeling so beaten down by others. There were obstacles about the class coming to fruition, and when I thought that the door was shut for good, God opened it, and I walked through it scared to death. The first ten months of 2022 were tough, to say the least. I also took an online class on the side and ordered a lot of books to read. But I made it through the class and clinicals and gained my FP-C, Certified Flight Paramedic. It was another fulfilling milestone when I passed that exam, but I have been very hesitant about getting a job. I still feel some self-doubt and fear of working with a person who may not be a good fit for me.

I have been continually asking God to direct my path and make it clear on the direction I should take. I am trying to have blind faith and remember the verse from day 3 taken from Jeremiah 29:11:

> For I know the plans I have for you, declares
> the Lord, plans to prosper you and not harm you,
> plans to give you hope and a future. (NIV)

I can assure you this has been a difficult journey for me. But I have learned some valuable lessons about jumping into something without God. He pruned me in many ways in 2022. I sold my motorcycle and my beloved 1952 Chevy pickup so I could go back to school. With only one income, we had to pick and choose what we could do. But God always provided us with just enough when we needed it. I am currently in contact with a company about a part-time job, and I am letting God lead me, because I do not want to make another mistake that may lead me down a path of destruction like before. I will just wait patiently and see what door God opens. Oddly enough, I am at peace in whatever direction He wants me to go.

Do you jump in headfirst on doing something without asking God first? If so, how did it turn out?

Do you have a desire for knowledge, or are you comfortable where you are?

Are you teachable in the ways of God?

I remember soaking God's Word up like a sponge when I became a believer. I read, listened, and studied. That's why I went to seminary. I just could not get enough of learning about Him. But when those wilderness years came, I slowly quit reading and studying the Scripture. I just took His Word for granted, and it cost me in a terrible way. I definitely went through a fire, but it has purified me in areas that needed it. I still have areas that need to be pruned. I am hardheaded and stubborn, but I am gaining that desire and thirst again to study God's Word. You may not be like me in some areas of learning, but I beg you to read, study, and meditate on God's Word. Always continue your education with God. Never ever stop learning His ways, even when you feel like your whole world has caved in around you. I know how deep and dark those valleys are, and I will forever regret not staying in His Word during those times.

DAY 25

Horse Tales

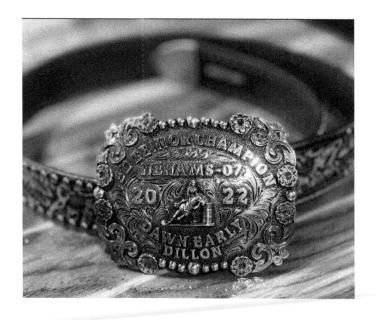

And let us consider how we may spur one another
on toward love and good deeds.
—Hebrews 10:24 NIV

After all the things I have gone through over the past few years, my friend circle is very small now. As mentioned, some people run for the hills when you need help. But I am very fortunate that I have a core group of people who love and encourage me in different areas.

Every one of them is uniquely special to me. But one in particular spurred me straight into an outlandish crazy adventure to barrel race again. Our debut was the last weekend of 2021, and I have already told you about what a fiasco that was. Here we both were over fifty and literally starting from the bottom, but at least we could run in the senior class. The year 2022 was shaping up to be busy, to say the least. I had school and now learning a new horse with the added bonus of losing weight to balance better in the saddle.

Now for the record, my friend and her husband have ridden many a mile with Robby and me trail riding over the years. We have had some great adventures traveling with our horses. But she was pushing me out of my comfort zone. We had not really competed in that capacity in over twenty-five years. I will be honest, it scared me silly. I have had some bad experiences turning those cans over the years. Being bucked off in your fifties is not the same as in your twenties. But we set a goal, joined out local National Barrel Horse Association club, and hit the road with high hopes of winning a buckle and qualifying for the world show.

I learned pretty quick; I was not going to make it without my old faithful horse Dillon. Now I was hauling two horses and paying two entry fees. While learning how to ride Clyde, Dillon was consistently placing me in the points. We were not fast by any means, but we made every show and ran clean runs. I protected my fifty-year-old self as well with a helmet, magic seat, and rubber bands around my feet. My sweet husband did not compete; and he was my trainer, stable boy, and encourager the whole year. I politely asked him not to compete because I knew he would beat me. My friend and I ran neck and neck the whole year, and I only slipped by her due to her not being able to make one run. As Robby said so eloquently at the awards banquet, "We each go out there to win, but then we cheer each other on knowing they may beat our time." That night I received my very first belt buckle in my division, and I ugly-cried in front of everyone. I cried because I never thought I would win a buckle, but also because I had wanted my friend to win it too. After all, she was the instigator of this incredible adventure. I know how competitive she is, and this year I fully believe she and Robby will outrun me, but hopefully we will each place in a division. My friend and I both did qualify for the world show, and Clyde and I should be ready by then. Dillon is going back on the trails to live his best life. He reluctantly ran barrels for me, but he never once bucked or acted a fool at the shows. He is truly a special horse.

This adventure that my friend put us in brought a spark back into me. I had to ride more, haul more, and compete; but it brought me back into a large group of people again. For someone who had self-isolated the last three years, being in large group settings sent my anxiety into overdrive. God used her and two horses to get me back out into a large group setting. I have met a terrific group of people, and they have encouraged me throughout 2022. I may never run the fastest time or even place in the highest division, and that is okay with me. I just want to keep moving forward. I referenced Galatians 6:2 on day 17, and I encourage you to reread it. My friend helped me carry a burden of fear of people, and slowly over that year, God let me see good in people again. I pray I can honor both scriptures referenced today in the future.

Do you examine your friend base and make sure it is solid?

Do you have friends who may not believe in God but have stuck with you throughout a disastrous situation? If so, do you try to portray God with them?

Are you the type of friend who stands beside a friend in a time of need?

The experiences I have had with friends taught me that you can have acquaintances and you can have core friends. I have learned too that while I need to be friendly and show compassion to people, I have to be very careful with whom I invest my heart with wholeheartedly. Matthew 10:16 says,

> I am sending you out like sheep among wolves, therefore be as shrewd as snakes and as innocent as doves. (NIV)

There is a fine balance in that scripture, and I take it to heart. You do not have to share every single detail of your life to everyone you meet. Ask God to give you discernment on who your core friends are. I wish time and again I had prayed more about my friendships with people. I certainly do now.

DAY 26

A Marriage on the Rocks

So they are no longer two, but one flesh, Therefore what
God has joined together, let no one separate.
—Matthew 19:5 NIV

I have written throughout this devotional about Robby and me. I have shared his thoughts and tidbits about our marriage. I will give you more insight today on our thirty years of marriage. Just like everything in life, Satan can find the tiniest crack and slither in to cause catastrophic damage. As 1 Peter 5:8 states,

Your enemy the devil prowls around like
a roaring lion looking for someone to devour.
(NIV)

When that armor of God is not on, you will get hit hard. To Satan, we both looked like a tasty morsel to swallow whole. Naively, we had taken each other for granted.

I think back on those early years of how much fun we had with horses, softball games with our daughter, karate with our son, and traveling to explore new things. We sang together, we grew in God together, and things were good. I remember a lady telling us one time that she and her husband were joined at the hip and shared the same brain. That is how I thought of us. We were inseparable. Somewhere along the way in those wilderness years previously discussed, we started drifting in different directions. I cannot pinpoint an exact time, but one day it was like we were strangers in our own home. Robby's job was demanding, and I was starting over in a new profession. If we had been right with the Lord, we probably would have weathered the storm coming better. We went through that storm like two mice sharing a toothpick for a raft. I honestly do not know how we both did not drown.

I have to say this again, if it had not been for the roots we had planted years earlier with God, we would not have made it. Through all the fights, the hurtful words said or ignoring each other, there was still something there.

Do not think we did not try to work on our marriage; we did. We simply had not asked God's help in it. In 2018, we went to Colorado to a remote dude ranch to try to reconnect. It was isolated with no cell service. It was an extraordinary adventure with beautiful scenery, exquisite food, and some hard-core horseback riding. We slept out under the stars one night and looked at the vastness of the starry skies in awe. We both wanted to find that spark in us again. Robby wanted my smile and laughter back, and I wanted my sweet, humble man back. Those two people seemed to be gone forever. I remember at the end of our stay, I started to get more and more anxious of going back home. And I lashed out in anger over something ridiculously stupid because I knew the reality that we were returning home to. That's how we were existing. We would try to get away and reconnect, but we would have to return to the chaos. It was a vicious cycle. It seemed like every time we made a step forward, a problem would appear and set us back even further. I was mentally exhausted, and so was he. It felt like neither of us had the energy to fight each other anymore. We went through the motions because neither one of us could walk out the door and leave. And I am glad that did not happen.

For three years our marriage slowly deteriorated into a pile of rubble with deep-seated resentment on both sides. It was not a pretty picture, but we sure knew how to hide and mask our pain in front of others. I am appalled at how we Christians try to hide every bad moment and pretend that everything is perfect. The church is supposed to be a lighthouse guiding us into fellowship with one another, saving the lost, and mostly importantly reaching out to the ones suffering. I felt like I had nowhere to turn in the Christian world for counseling and help. So here we were just continually trying to kick our way out of quicksand, which makes you sink faster. We were trying to tie a knot in a rope and hang on to what we knew we could be again. But how to get there was going to be another long journey. Satan was trying hard to separate us.

Do you put God first in your marriage? Why or why not?

Do you think God should work on you or your spouse more?

How do you think the church handles people when they need help in their marriage? Does your church offer any kind of counseling services?

Are you scared people will gossip about you behind your back if they know you have problems of any kind?

I am going to answer the last one. Yes, there will be some talk. But I would rather have people talking instead of losing something good. I am so tired of putting on a brave face or trying to appear perfect. I am not perfect, but God tells us He loves us, and He wants us praying for one another. He wants us to go and talk to Him at the altar. And He wants us to reach out to others in a loving, compassionate way.

DAY 27

Finding us Again

Though one may be overpowered, two can defend themselves,
A cord of three strands is not quickly broken.
*   —Ecclesiastes 4:12 NIV*

I find this verse can be used in marriage or with friends. However Solomon intended for us to interpret this verse, He laid the foundation that a cord of three is strong. For me, I can apply this in my marriage. I believe the third strand with Robby and me is God. We have fully realized that just the two of us cannot maintain a healthy relationship without God. He is the thread that completes our strand of three. Braiding Him back into our lives has not been easy, but our braid is looking better and better. It is not the sloppy mess it has been over the last few years. You may ask how we were/are able to put the pieces back together, and all I can say is it has been a combination of small things.

For starters, we were back in church like we should have been. As stated before, we were back in church cautiously optimistic, but keeping the perspective real. I was not under the delusion that everything would go back the way they were years earlier. But I did have a spark of hope starting to bubble up. While the church we attended was without a full-time pastor at the time, we had some very good interim pastors who brought the Word back alive again. I still have not gone back into a Sunday school class, because I miss teaching so much. And I just have not felt comfortable in that type of group setting. But I have sat in the sanctuary and have had some wonderful talks and fellowship with two of those interims. They were both older pastors and had the maturity I needed to transition back into church. Each was very different in their personalities, but equally sound in the Scriptures. There were no judgments, just honest dialogue.

Outside of church, we were learning how to communicate again without getting into an argument. We were working on the restoration of the Airstream during that time, and we were making plans again about places we wanted to go and see. We were trail riding with friends who knew what we had been through. It was nice not having to explain myself or be on my guard with them. Those road trips we took were good for us. We could get away and start reconnecting. Our first trip out in Stella Rose, we went to Albuquerque, New Mexico, with both dogs. It was an eventful trip for sure. One dog traveled well in a vehicle, and the other threw up every time we made over three turns in a row. We tried Dramamine, but it really did not help much. We just learned to drive slower around the turns. But they were great to blunder around with and camp with. We enjoyed visiting Albuquerque and Santa Fe again. We took long walks around the campground, shopped, and laughed at silly things. I enjoyed the trip back, because I finally convinced Robby we could pull over in a truck stop or a rest area and catch some sleep on the way home. He did not believe he would be able to sleep due to the noise. He did. It was a good week of reconnecting, and we really started looking forward to future adventures.

We started making some improvements around the house and planning things that needed to get done later. It was those little, tiny baby steps of everyday life that were drawing us back together. There was no single defining moment that told us everything was going to work out. Just like there was no single moment when everything fell apart. I am still guarded in some areas as I am sure he is. But we are finally on the right path. And the right path started when we put God back in our lives and our marriage. I do not think we would have made it if Robby had not gotten that phone call asking him to come back to that church.

Robby's thoughts on reconnecting are as follows:

> Being understanding and accepting what is available. Meaning sometimes either one of us has to be able to accept whatever the other is able to give. The factor for me to start building a better relationship were our wedding vows, which state for better or worse in sickness and in health. I could not just take the good and give up during the bad.

Do you believe your marriage is a cord of three strands? If not, why?

If you are struggling in your marriage, what first attracted you to your spouse? Can you remember the fun times before things fell apart?

Do you cherish your wedding vows and take them to heart?

The best wedding anniversary present my husband ever gave me was the gift of renewing our vows. For our tenth wedding anniversary, he took me to the church, and it was just us and the preacher. There were no nerves involved in that ceremony. We laughed like two teenagers in love. It was the sweetest moment for us, and I intend to pray for those precious simple moments in the future. I think sometimes we forget the simplicity of life. We both took an oath to cherish each other twice, and somehow it got lost in the chaos, but I am ready for some of those beautiful simple moments again.

DAY 28

Forgiving Does Not Mean Forgetting

For if you forgive men when they sin against you, your
heavenly Father will also forgive you. But if you do not forgive
men their sins, your Father will not forgive your sins.
—Matthew 6:14–15 NIV

Be kind and compassionate to one another, forgiving
each other, just as in Christ God forgave you.
—Ephesians 4:32 NIV

This is the day to address the elephant in the room. How do we forgive ourselves and others? For a long time after my suicide attempt,
I will admit that sometimes anger was the only thing I could cling
on to. I absolutely did not want to feel the rawness of my pain. And
I knew whenever I let go of the anger, that is what I would feel. I did
not want to forgive anyone including myself. When anger is rooted
deep inside of us, it affects every aspect of your life. And if you do
not let it go, it not only affects you emotionally and physically, but
affects everyone around you as well. You do not like yourself, and it
causes people to avoid you. They get tired of hearing about what you
are angry about.

The moment came when I finally just had to start letting it go.
God was letting me see beauty again, and I did not want to mess it up.
Letting go of the anger I had and forgiving the hurts from the past

five years was instrumental in my complete healing. The first step I took was I went back one Sunday to the church where I had learned and grew in God. It was not easy, but it helped me gain some closure. I felt like if I went back to where my journey with God began, I could move forward in the forgiveness area. My mind was flooded with so many memories. I thought about Robby and me being baptized there and my children as well. I thought about all the joy and laughter that was shared there through Vacation Bible School, revivals, fellowship meals, and trips with the youth. Those were special times in my life. I also realized that day that there could be special times in ministry again. I just had to let all that anger and bitterness go, and I did. Has it bubbled up occasionally since then? Absolutely! Then I just look up and ask God to please continue working in my life. I ask Him to let me maintain compassion for others. I ask Him to let me find peace from all the hurt.

I realize that there will always be sadness about losing people. I know from time to time bad memories will resurface. I will never forget what happened to me, but I am forgiving the hurts from others. Also, I am learning to forgive myself from my transgressions. I do not want to play the victim or be a victim. I cannot control other people, only myself. I am trying to take a step back and ask God how I should handle difficult moments. I am trying to see others through their eyes. As stated, people hide behind masks, so we do not always know why people act the way they do. God has forgiven me more times than I can count. I do not know how He forgives and shows so much compassion for us, but I pray that he can guide me in that area. I do not want to experience all that anger inside me again. Satan held me in that season for way too long. I am ready for a season of peace, laughter, and healing.

Ephesians 4:32 in the Amplified Bible reads like this:

> Be kind and helpful to one another, tender-hearted [compassionate, understanding], forgiving one another [readily and freely] just as God in Christ also forgave you.

The words *tender-hearted*, *readily*, and *freely* literally leap off the page at me. I am so glad my heart is not petrified now. But accepting those words on how to forgive makes me cringe. God has forgiven all my transgressions readily and freely. Whew! Friends, He wants us to forgive the same way. That takes some altar praying, and I have taken it to the altar.

Do you freely forgive, or is it begrudgingly?

When you think about the things God forgives for, how does it make you feel?

Do your knees need to be by that altar on Sundays?

For me to follow that command, I must meditate on His Word, pray frequently, and humble myself to walk down and kneel at the altar. That is so hard for a Christian to do. I think we are missing out on a lot of blessings by not taking our hurts, anger, and worries to the altar. We have too much pride, people!

1 Peter 5:6–7 says,

> Humble yourselves, therefore under God's mighty hand, that he may lift you up in due time. Cast all your anxiety on him because he cares for you. (NIV)

DAY 29

Stopping Satan through the Word

Jesus said to him, "Away from me, Satan! For it is written:
Worship the Lord your God and serve him only." Then the
devil left him, and angels came and attended him.
—Matthew 4:10–11 NIV

I heard Matthew 4:1–11 preached on recently, and the devil tempting Jesus gives a clear and profound answer on defeating Satan. While on earth, Jesus was tempted, hated, and tormented just like we are. He did not have an easy thirty-three years on this earth. But he gave us instructions on how to handle so many situations in life. As I have been writing this, I have rediscovered so many golden nuggets in the Scripture. There are so many I wanted to reference, but I feel God gave me the ones for this journey.

Satan's temptation of Jesus in the wilderness happened at His weakest moment. After fasting for forty days, He was weak and tired, and He still defeated Satan. Every time He was tempted, He quoted the Scripture. I do not know about you, but when I was in my wilderness journey, I was not quoting the Scripture. Quite the opposite, in fact. I was so far away from God, my Bible was gathering dust. That is so hard to admit. We as Christians seem to have a problem admitting we do not pray enough or read the Scripture enough. I love the old Southern saying, "I grew up in the church, so I know what is in the Bible." But are you living your life like the Bible says to?

There was no way I was going to stop Satan on my own. But I kept ignoring all the signs God was giving me. I was ignoring what my husband was telling me, and he was ignoring what I was telling him I saw in him. That is how Satan works. He causes so much confusion that we are blinded by the truth. Darkness is in our path, and we cannot see in the dark unless we have a light. For Christians, that light is Jesus. I cannot understand how we the church are ignoring our responsibility to help each other in times of crisis. We are supposed to be a sanctuary for all. After my experience in the wilderness, I cannot understand how we are so arrogant in our walk with God. I have been so broken that my prayer is "God, please do not let arrogance take over me." I know there will be other trials and temptations, but I am claiming that verse in Matthew 4:10. I want Satan gone, and the only way I can keep him at bay is to serve God the best I can. Some days I am sure I will fail and fall on my face. But while I am down there, I will be praying for the strength to overcome.

If Satan starts taking root in any situation, please start praying and reading the Word. If you do not, you may fall in that slimy pit like I did. And believe me it is not any fun at all. It almost destroyed me, and you do not want to know that feeling.

Do you believe you can rebuke Satan?

Do you realize the suffering you cause to others and God by not following Jesus's example?

Do you have certain scriptures you can quote when you are tempted by Satan?

The wilderness is a lonely, desolate place. You are tired mentally, spiritually, and physically. The only way you will survive is through the Word of God. Thankfully, I had people who were praying for me when I could not. It is a true miracle I am here today. I should be dead. It weighs heavy on my heart that I got to that point. It is a heavy burden to bear that I caused the people who love me so much pain. But I am still here; and three years after my suicide attempt, I am rediscovering my walk with God, myself, and my husband. I still have a lot more to work on to feel whole again. But I am wholeheartedly trying.

DAY 30

Tidbits for Trouble

Peace I leave with you; my peace I give you. I do not give to you as the world gives. Do not let your heart be troubled and do not be afraid.
—John 14:27 NIV

Let the peace of Christ rule in your hearts, since as members
of one body you were called to peace. And be thankful.
—Colossians 3:15 NIV

Each one should use whatever gift he has received to serve others,
faithfully administering God's grace in its various forms.
—1 Peter 4:10 NIV

Humble yourselves before the Lord, and he will lift you up.
—James 4:10 NIV

Today is the last day of this journey with you. I have poured so much of myself into this devotional, and if it helps one person, that will be a blessing to me. No two people will follow the same exact path. We will have people travel with us for a while, and then there is a cross-road, and you go in different directions. There are chance encounters, lasting impressions made by others, journeys with the wrong people, and journeys with the right people. Our journeys may be different, but we will all experience joy, sadness, anger, hurt, trials, temptations, and any other emotion you can think of. I am going to list some things that continue to help me on mine and maybe help on your journey.

Recognize each season you are in.

If a situation does not feel safe, get out!

Listen to the ones who have your best interest at heart.

Do not let Satan take root.

Understand that not everyone will be in your life forever. It may hurt to have to cut ties with someone, but not everyone is right for you.

Let go of anger and bitterness. It will destroy you.

Find a sanctuary to retreat to when you need to verbally tell your troubles to God.

Love the ones who love you. Even if you feel unlovable, a hug from a spouse or friend helps.

Spend time with the ones who uplift you. I have friends whom I go out and eat with, and I love when we eat Italian. I have friends

I ride horses with. I have friends whom I enjoy the symphony with or go and eat at their house. The food is spectacular there. You get the meaning here. It is not the quantity but the quality of friends you have.

Help others when the Spirit directs you. Remember you cannot help everyone.

Focus on God first.

If a relationship needs mending, then work hard on it. I am glad Robby and I are working on ours. But it takes two willing people. Either one of us could have walked away, but we hung on.

Pray for the church.

And please, if you ever have suicidal ideations, call the national suicide hotline 988.

Call 911 but get help.

Please do not bully anyone. And recognize when you are being bullied and just walk away. Your mental health is worth it.

Concentrate on the verses today and strive to live like Jesus. Pray and read the Scripture!

I have a personal list of things I need to work on, as I am sure you do. I have personal needs that I pray God will provide for me. I came through this battle with a lot of internal scars, and going forward, I pray I recognize the signs of Satan stirring in my business early on. Walking in the dark was terrifying and lonely. I do not want to feel that depth of darkness again. You do not either.

I stumbled across these words from J. R. R. Tolkien taken from *The Fellowship of the Ring*:

> The world is indeed full of peril, and in it there are many dark places; But still there is much that is fair, and though in all lands love is now mingled with grief, it grows perhaps the greater.

I leave you with this from 1 Corinthians 13:4–7 (NIV):

> Love is patient, love is kind. It does not envy, it does not boast, it is not proud. It does not dishonor others, it is not self-seeking, it is not easily angered, it keeps no record of wrongs. Love does not delight in evil but rejoices with the truth. It always protects, always trusts, always hopes, always perseveres.

I would encourage you to read all of chapter 13. I pray your journey is filled with love and that you stay under the protection of God. Put God's armor on and do not let Satan defeat you, and find sanctuary in the Lord.

ABOUT THE AUTHOR

Dawn Early is a simple Southern girl from Mississippi trying to navigate through the twists and turns of her journey while here on earth. She is an avid photographer and nature lover. If she is not seeing the world from the back of a horse, she is walking the woods and creek with her two dogs and cat. She has a heart for missions and has traveled to three different countries helping others in the name of Christ. She has her two-year certificate in biblical teaching through Leavell College, which is in affiliation with New Orleans Baptist Theological Seminary. Dawn is a paramedic, who recently obtained her Certified Flight Paramedic (FP-C). As of now, she is allowing the Holy Spirit to direct her future endeavors. She and her husband enjoy traveling with their horses and friends, trail riding, and barrel racing. They especially love camping in their renovated 1966 Airstream. While she loves her family and friends with all her heart, she knows that her relationship with God must come first. She has learned the hard way that without God being front and center, the journey of life can get very dark. She has failed many times as a Christian, but she is constantly striving to improve herself. She fully believes that light always overcomes darkness, good triumphs over evil, and love overcomes hate.

Milton Keynes UK
Ingram Content Group UK Ltd.
UKHW022219070923
428268UK00005B/58